Modern Critical Interpretations

Modern Critical Interpretations

A Scholarly Look at
The Diary of Anne Frank

Edited and with an introduction by
Harold Bloom
Sterling Professor of the Humanities
Yale University

CHELSEA HOUSE PUBLISHERS
Philadelphia

© 1999 by Chelsea House Publishers, a subsidiary of
Haights Cross Communications.

Introduction © 1999 by Harold Bloom

Printed and bound in the United States of America

10 9 8 7 6 5 4 3 2

∞ The paper used in this publication meets the minimum
requirements of the American National Standard for
Permanence of Paper for Printed Library Materials,
Z39.48-1984

Library of Congress Cataloging-in-Publication Data

A scholarly look at The diary of Anne Frank / edited and
with an introduction by Harold Bloom.
        cm. – (Modern critical interpretations)
     Includes bibliographical references and index.
     ISBN 0-7910-5192-7 (hardcover)
     1. Frank, Anne, 1929-1945.   Achterhuis.
   2. Holocaust, 1939-1945—Psychological aspects.
   3. Holocaust, Jewish (1939-1945)—Influence.
   I. Bloom, Harold.   II. Series.
DS135.N6F7356   1998
940.53'18'092—dc21   [b]   98-49479
                                               CIP

Contributing Editor: Tenley Williams

Contents

Editor's Note

My Introduction centers upon a remarkable fantasy of Nathan Zuckerman's, in Philip Roth's *The Ghost Writer*, where a young woman, Amy Bellette, suffers the delusion of believing that *she is* Anne Frank.

Since *The Diary of Anne Frank* is more of a historical emblem than a literary work, the essays are essentially exercises in morality and history.

Bruno Bettelheim, whose work as a child psychologist now seems questionable to many, argues that the fame of the book, the play, and the motion picture *The Diary of Anne Frank* have worked to obscure what Bettelheim considers the poor judgment of the Frank family.

Lawrence L. Langer faults the play and film based upon the diary for evading a fuller representation of the Holocaust.

To Yasmine Ergas, *The Diary of Anne Frank* resonates in our memory, while Sander L. Gilman, partly through the lens of Roth's *The Ghost Writer*, sees the *Diary* and its offshoots as "providing the matrix for a discussion of the appropriate language of the Jew as survivor."

Anne Frank's reading, which included Thackeray and Oscar Wilde, is set forth by Sylvia Patterson Iskander, who also attempts an analysis of Anne Frank's style.

Whether nightmare and Anne Frank's wistfulness can coexist is considered by Barbara Chiarello, in a gallant effort of an essay, while Molly Magid Hoagland contrasts the *Diary* and the play.

This volume culminates with a passionate essay by the distinguished Jewish writer, Cynthia Ozick, who bitterly contests the usurpation of the *Diary* by all those who "have contributed to the conversion of Anne Frank into usable goods."

Introduction

In Philip Roth's accomplished novel, *The Ghost Writer*, there is a remarkable fantasy that could be called "The Return of Anne Frank." Nathan Zuckerman, the portrait of the artist Philip Roth as a young man, stays overnight at the home of the Jewish novelist Lonoff (taken by some as a version of Bernard Malamud, but actually a composite figure). Also in the house is a mysterious young woman, Amy Bellette. In Nathan's imagination she is the actual Anne Frank, who somehow survived the death camp and now lives incognito as Lonoff's assistant. Amy denies having read Anne Frank's *Diary*, which inspires Nathan to an eloquent description of the book:

> She was a marvelous young writer. She was something for thirteen. It's like watching an accelerated film of a fetus sprouting a face, watching her mastering things . . . Suddenly, she's discovering reflection, suddenly there's portraiture, character sketches, suddenly there's long intricate eventful happening so beautifully recounted it seems to have gone through a dozen drafts. And no poisonous notion of being *interesting* or *serious*. She just *is*.

This remains the most accurate tribute to the *Diary*, at least that I've encountered. A child's diary, even when she was so natural a writer, rarely could sustain literary criticism. Since *this* diary is emblematic of hundreds of thousands of murdered children, criticism is irrelevant. I myself have no special qualifications except as a literary critic. One cannot write about Anne Frank's *Diary* as if Shakespeare, or Philip Roth, is the subject. Jewish cultural survival is a complex problem, involving as it does issues of memory, discontinuity, and bad faith. I cannot see any authentic relationship between the poignance the *Diary* necessarily had acquired, and the burdens of American Jewish culture. Therefore I will confine my own observations on the *Diary* to my Editor's Note, where I consider the reactions of others, from Bruno

Bettelheim, an equivocal healer, to Cynthia Ozick, a distinguished writer of fictions. In the remainder of this Introduction, I will return to Nathan Zuckerman's vision of Anne Frank, largely because, as a literary critic, I judge Philip Roth to be one of the handful of novelists now at work in the United States who will matter most to posterity. The author of *Zuckerman Bound*, *Operation Shylock*, *Sabbath's Theater,* and *American Pastoral* is of the eminence shared by Thomas Pynchon, Don De Lillo, and Cormac McCarthy. Roth's sense of Anne Frank, or rather of her image, should help the rest of us to clarify our own relation to that image.

In *Reading Myself and Others* (1985), Roth, interviewed by Hermione Lee, remarks that: "It wasn't easy to see that Amy Bellette as Anne Frank was Zuckerman's own creation." He later expanded upon this difficulty:

> I had trouble getting that right. When I began, in the third person, I was somehow *revering* the material. I was taking a high elegiac tone in telling the story of Anne Frank surviving and coming to America. I didn't know where I was going so I began by doing what you're supposed to do when writing the life of a saint. It was the tone appropriate to hagiography. Instead of Anne Frank gaining new meaning within the context of my story, I was trying to draw from the ready store of stock emotions that everybody is supposed to have about her. It's what even good actors sometimes will do during the first weeks of rehearsing a play—gravitate to the conventional form of presentation, cling to the cliché while anxiously waiting for something authentic to take hold. In retrospect, my difficulties look somewhat bizarre, because just what Zuckerman was fighting against, I was in fact succumbing to—the officially authorized and most consoling legend. I tell you, no one who later complained that in *The Ghost Writer* I had abused the memory of Anne Frank would have batted an eye had I let those banalities out into the world. That would have been just fine; I might even have got a citation. But I couldn't have given myself any prizes for it. The difficulties of telling a Jewish story—How should it be told? In what tone? To whom should it be told? To what end? Should it be told at all?— were finally to become *The Ghost Writer's* theme. But before it became a theme, it apparently had to be an ordeal. It often happens, at least with me, that the struggles that generate a book's moral life are naively enacted upon the body of the book during the early, uncertain stages of writing. That is the ordeal,

and it ended when I took that whole section and recast it in the first person—Anne Frank's story told by Amy Bellette. The victim wasn't herself going to talk about her plight in the voice of "The March of Time." She hadn't in the *Diary*, so why should she in life? I didn't want this section to *appear* as first-person narration, but I knew that by passing it through the first-person sieve, I stood a good chance of getting rid of this terrible tone, which wasn't hers, but mine. I did get rid of it. The impassioned cadences, the straining emotions, the somber, overdramatized, archaic diction—I cleared it all out, thanks to Amy Bellette. Rather straightforwardly, I then cast the section *back* into the third person, and then I was able to get to work on it—to write rather than to rhapsodize or eulogize.

Amy Bellette's story, precisely because it is *not* Anne Frank's, but a fictive revision, is refreshingly free of the cadences of a saint's life. And of course, Amy's story is a passionate lie, "her consuming delusion," akin to Nathan Zuckerman's mad ambition somehow to marry Anne Frank, by distracting Amy away from her obsession with Lonoff. What Philip Roth accomplishes, here as with his broodings on Kafka, is not a reimagining of Anne Frank, but a heightening of our awareness of how difficult it has become to tell *any* Jewish story, this late in so long and so complex a cultural history.

BRUNO BETTELHEIM

The Ignored Lesson of Anne Frank

When the world first learned about the Nazi concentration and death camps, most civilized people felt the horrors committed in them to be so uncanny as to be unbelievable. It came as a severe shock that supposedly civilized nations could stoop to such inhuman acts. The implication that modern man has such inadequate control over his cruel and destructive proclivities was felt as a threat to our views of ourselves and our humanity. Three different psychological mechanisms were most frequently used for dealing with the appalling revelation of what had gone on in the camps:

> (1) its applicability to man in general was denied by asserting—contrary to evidence—that the acts of torture and mass murder were committed by a small group of insane or perverted persons;
>
> (2) the truth of the reports was denied by declaring them vastly exaggerated and ascribing them to propaganda (this originated with the German government, which called all reports on terror in the camps "horror propaganda"—*Greuelpropaganda*);
>
> (3) the reports were believed, but the knowledge of the horror repressed as soon as possible.

From *Surviving and Other Essays.* © 1979 by Bruno Bettelheim and Trude Bettelheim as Trustees. Reprinted by permission of Alfred A. Knopf, Inc.

All three mechanisms could be seen at work after liberation of those prisoners remaining. At first, after the discovery of the camps and their death-dealing, a wave of extreme outrage swept the Allied nations. It was soon followed by a general repression of the discovery in people's minds. Possibly this reaction was due to something more than the blow dealt to modern man's narcissism by the realization that cruelty is still rampant among men. Also present may have been the dim but extremely threatening realization that the modern state now has available the means for changing personality, and for destroying millions it deems undesirable. The ideas that in our day a people's personalities might be changed against their will by the state, and that other populations might be wholly or partially exterminated, are so fearful that one tries to free oneself of them and their impact by defensive denial, or by repression.

The extraordinary world-wide success of the book, play, and movie *The Diary of Anne Frank* suggests the power of the desire to counteract the realization of the personality-destroying and murderous nature of the camps by concentrating all attention on what is experienced as a demonstration that private and intimate life can continue to flourish even under the direct persecution by the most ruthless totalitarian system. And this although Anne Frank's fate demonstrates how efforts at disregarding in private life what goes on around one in society can hasten one's own destruction.

What concerns me here is not what actually happened to the Frank family, how they tried—and failed—to survive their terrible ordeal. It would be very wrong to take apart so humane and moving a story, which aroused so much well-merited compassion for gentle Anne Frank and her tragic fate. What is at issue is the universal and uncritical response to her diary and to the play and movie based on it, and what this reaction tells about our attempts to cope with the feelings her fate—used by us to serve as a symbol of a most human reaction to Nazi terror—arouses in us. I believe that the world-wide acclaim given her story cannot be explained unless we recognize in it our wish to forget the gas chambers, and our effort to do so by glorifying the ability to retreat into an extremely private, gentle, sensitive world, and there to cling as much as possible to what have been one's usual daily attitudes and activities, although surrounded by a maelstrom apt to engulf one at any moment.

The Frank family's attitude that life could be carried on as before may well have been what led to their destruction. By eulogizing how they lived in their hiding place while neglecting to examine first whether it was a reasonable or an effective choice, we are able to ignore the crucial lesson of their story—that such an attitude can be fatal in extreme circumstances..

While the Franks were making their preparations for going passively into hiding, thousands of other Jews in Holland (as elsewhere in Europe) were trying to escape to the free world, in order to survive and/or fight. Others who could not escape went underground—into hiding—each family member with, for example, a different gentile family. We gather from the diary, however, that the chief desire of the Frank family was to continue living as nearly as possible in the same fashion to which they had been accustomed in happier times.

Little Anne, too, wanted only to go on with life as usual, and what else could she have done but fall in with the pattern her parents created for her existence? But hers was not a necessary fate, much less a heroic one; it was a terrible but also a senseless fate. Anne had a good chance to survive, as did many Jewish children in Holland. But she would have had to leave her parents and go to live with a gentile Dutch family, posing as their own child, something her parents would have had to arrange for her.

Everyone who recognized the obvious knew that the hardest way to go underground was to do it as a family; to hide out together made detection by the SS most likely; and when detected, everybody was doomed. By hiding singly, even when one got caught, the others had a chance to survive. The Franks, with their excellent connections among gentile Dutch families, might well have been able to hide out singly, each with a different family. But instead, the main principle of their planning was continuing their beloved family life—an understandable desire, but highly unrealistic in those times. Choosing any other course would have meant not merely giving up living together, but also realizing the full measure of the danger to their lives.

The Franks were unable to accept that going on living as a family as they had done before the Nazi invasion of Holland was no longer a desirable way of life, much as they loved each other; in fact, for them and others like them, it was a most dangerous behavior. But even given their wish not to separate, they failed to make appropriate preparations for what was likely to happen.

There is little doubt that the Franks, who were able to provide themselves with so much while arranging for going into hiding, and even while hiding, could have provided themselves with some weapons had they wished. Had they had a gun, Mr. Frank could have shot down at least one or two of the "green police" who came for them. There was no surplus of such police, and the loss of an SS with every Jew arrested would have noticeably hindered the functioning of the police state. Even a butcher knife, which they certainly could have taken with them into hiding, could have been used by them in self-defense. The fate of the Franks wouldn't have been very different, because they all died anyway except for Anne's father. But they could have sold their lives for a high price, instead of walking to their death. Still, although one must assume that Mr. Frank would have fought courageously, as we know he did when a soldier in the first World War, it is not everybody who can plan to kill those who are bent on killing him, although many who would not be ready to contemplate doing so would be willing to kill those who are bent on murdering not only them but also their wives and little daughters.

An entirely different matter would have been planning for escape in case of discovery. The Franks' hiding place had only one entrance; it did not have any other exit. Despite this fact, during their many months of hiding, they did not try to devise one. Nor did they make other plans for escape, such as that one of the family members—as likely as not Mr. Frank—would try to detain the police in the narrow entrance way—maybe even fight them, as suggested above—thus giving other members of the family a chance to escape, either by reaching the roofs of adjacent houses, or down a ladder into the alley behind the house in which they were living.

Any of this would have required recognizing and accepting the desperate straits in which they found themselves, and concentrating on how best to cope with them. This was quite possible to do, even under the terrible conditions in which the Jews found themselves after the Nazi occupation of Holland. It can be seen from many other accounts, for example from the story of Marga Minco, a girl of about Anne Frank's age who lived to tell about it. Her parents had planned that when the police should come for them, the father would try to detain them by arguing and fighting with them, to give the wife and daughter a chance to escape through a rear door. Unfortunately it did not quite work out this way, and both parents got killed. But their short-lived resistance permitted their daughter to make her escape as planned and to reach a Dutch family who saved her.

This is not mentioned as a criticism that the Frank family did not plan or behave along similar lines. A family has every right to arrange their life as they wish or think best, and to take the risks they want to take. My point is not to criticize what the Franks did, but only the universal admiration of their way of coping, or rather of not coping. The story of little Marga who survived, every bit as touching, remains totally neglected by comparison.

Many Jews—unlike the Franks, who through listening to British radio news were better informed than most—had no detailed knowledge of the extermination camps. Thus it was easier for them to make themselves believe that complete compliance with even the most outrageously debilitating and degrading Nazi orders might offer a chance for survival. But neither tremendous anxiety that inhibits clear thinking and with it well-planned and determined action, nor ignorance about what happened to those who responded with passive waiting for being rounded up for their extermination, can explain the reaction of audiences to the play and movie retelling Anne's story, which are all about such waiting that results finally in destruction.

I think it is the fictitious ending that explains the enormous success of this play and movie. At the conclusion we hear Anne's voice from the beyond, saying, "In spite of everything, I still believe that people are really good at heart." This improbable sentiment is supposedly from a girl who had been starved to death, had watched her sister meet the same fate before she did, knew that her mother had been murdered, and had watched untold thousands of adults and children being killed. This statement is not justified by anything Anne actually told her diary.

Going on with intimate family living, no matter how dangerous it might be to survival, was fatal to all too many during the Nazi regime. And if all men are good, then indeed we can all go on with living our lives as we have been accustomed to in times of undisturbed safety and can afford to forget about Auschwitz. But Anne, her sister, her mother, may well have died because her parents could not get themselves to believe in Auschwitz.

While play and movie are ostensibly about Nazi persecution and destruction, in actuality what we watch is the way that, despite this terror, lovable people manage to continue living their satisfying intimate lives with each other. The heroine grows from a child into a young adult as normally as any other girl would, despite the most abnormal conditions of all other aspects of her existence, and that of her family. Thus the play reassures us that despite the destructiveness of Nazi racism and tyranny in general, it is possible to disregard it in one's private life much of the time, even if one is Jewish.

True, the ending happens just as the Franks and their friends had feared all along: their hiding place is discovered, and they are carried away to their doom. But the fictitious declaration of faith in the goodness of all men which concludes the play falsely reassures us since it impresses on us that in the combat between Nazi terror and continuance of intimate family living the latter wins out, since Anne has the last word. This is simply contrary to fact, because it was she who got killed. Her seeming survival through her moving statement about the goodness of men releases us effectively of the need to cope with the problems Auschwitz presents. That is why we are so relieved by her statement. It explains why millions loved play and movie, because while it confronts us with the fact that Auschwitz existed it encourages us at the same time to ignore any of its implications. If all men are good at heart, there never really was an Auschwitz; nor is there any possibility that it may recur.

The desire of Anne Frank's parents not to interrupt their intimate family living, and their inability to plan more effectively for their survival, reflect the failure of all too many others faced with the threat of Nazi terror. It is a failure that deserves close examination because of the inherent warnings it contains for us, the living.

Submission to the threatening power of the Nazi state often led both to the disintegration of what had once seemed well-integrated personalities and to a return to an immature disregard for the dangers of reality. Those Jews who submitted passively to Nazi persecution came to depend on primitive and infantile thought processes: wishful thinking and disregard for the possibility of death. Many persuaded themselves that they, out of all the others, would be spared. Many more simply disbelieved in the possibility of their own death. Not believing it, they did not take what seemed to them desperate precautions, such as giving up everything to hide out singly; or trying to escape even if it meant risking their lives in doing so; or preparing to fight for their lives when no escape was possible and death had become an immediate possibility. It is true that defending their lives in active combat before they were rounded up to be transported into the camps might have hastened their deaths, and so, up to a point, they were protecting themselves by "rolling with the punches" of the enemy.

But the longer one rolls with the punches dealt not by the normal vagaries of life, but by one's eventual executioner, the more likely it becomes that one will no longer have the strength to resist when death becomes imminent. This is particularly true if yielding to the enemy is accompanied not by a commensurate strengthening of the personality, but by an inner disintegration. We can observe such a process among the Franks, who bickered with each other over trifles, instead of supporting each other's ability to resist the demoralizing impact of their living conditions.

Those who faced up to the announced intentions of the Nazis prepared for the worst as a real and imminent possibility. It meant risking one's life for a self-chosen purpose, but in doing so, creating at least a small chance for saving one's own life or those of others, or both. When Jews in Germany were restricted to their homes, those who did not succumb to inertia took the new restrictions as a warning that it was high time to go underground, join the resistance movement, provide themselves with forged papers, and so on, if they had not done so long ago. Many of them survived.

Some distant relatives of mine may furnish an example. Early in the war, a young man living in a small Hungarian town banded together with a number of other Jews to prepare against a German invasion. As soon as the Nazis imposed curfews on the Jews, his group left for Budapest—because the bigger capital city with its greater anonymity offered chances for escaping detection. Similar groups from other towns converged in Budapest and joined forces. From among themselves they selected typically "Aryan" looking men who equipped themselves with false papers and immediately joined the Hungarian SS. These spies were then able to warn of impending persecution and raids.

Many of these groups survived intact. Furthermore, they had also equipped themselves with small arms, so that if they were detected, they could put up enough of a fight for the majority to escape while a few would die fighting to make the escape possible. A few of the Jews who had joined the SS were discovered and immediately shot, probably a death preferable to one in the gas chambers. But most of even these Jews survived, hiding within the SS until liberation.

Compare these arrangements not just to the Franks' selection of a hiding place that was basically a trap without an outlet but with Mr. Frank's teaching typically academic high-school subjects to his children rather than how to make a getaway: a token of his inability to face the seriousness of the threat of death. Teaching high-school subjects had, of course, its constructive aspects. It relieved the ever-present anxiety about their fate to some degree by concentrating on different matters, and by implication it encouraged hope for a future in which such knowledge would be useful. In this sense such teaching was purposeful, but it was erroneous in that it took the place of much more pertinent teaching and planning: how best to try to escape when detected.

Unfortunately the Franks were by no means the only ones who, out of anxiety, became unable to contemplate their true situation and with it to plan accordingly. Anxiety, and the wish to counteract it by clinging to each other, and to reduce its sting by continuing as much as possible with their usual way of life incapacitated many, particularly when survival plans required changing radically old ways of living that they cherished, and which had become their only source of satisfaction.

My young relative, for example, was unable to persuade other members of his family to go with him when he left the small town where he had lived with them. Three times, at tremendous risk to himself, he returned to plead with his relatives, pointing out first the growing persecution of the Jews, and later the fact that transport to the gas chambers had already begun. He could not convince these Jews to leave their homes and break up their families to go singly into hiding.

As their desperation mounted, they clung more determinedly to their old living arrangements and to each other, became less able to consider giving up the possessions they had accumulated through hard work over a lifetime. The more severely their freedom to act was reduced, and what little they were still permitted to do restricted by insensible and degrading regulations imposed by the Nazis, the more did they become unable to contemplate independent action. Their life energies drained out of them, sapped by their ever-greater anxiety. The less they found strength in themselves, the more they held on to the little that was left of what had given them security in the past—their old surroundings, their customary way of life, their possessions—all these seemed to give their lives some permanency, offer some symbols of security. Only what had once been symbols of security now endangered life, since they were excuses for avoiding change. On each successive visit the young man found his relatives more incapacitated, less willing or able to take his advice, more frozen into inactivity, and with it further along the way to the crematoria where, in fact, they all died.

Levin renders a detailed account of the desperate but fruitless efforts made by small Jewish groups determined to survive to try to save the rest.

She tells how messengers were "sent into the provinces to warn Jews that deportation meant death, but their warnings were ignored because most Jews refused to contemplate their own annihilation." I believe the reason for such refusal has to be found in their inability to take action. If we are certain that we are helpless to protect ourselves against the danger of destruction, we cannot contemplate it. We can consider the danger only as long as we believe there are ways to protect ourselves, to fight back, to escape. If we are convinced none of this is possible for us, then there is no point in thinking about the danger; on the contrary, it is best to refuse to do so.

As a prisoner in Buchenwald, I talked to hundreds of German Jewish prisoners who were brought there as part of the huge pogrom in the wake of the murder of vom Rath in the fall of 1938. I asked them why they had not left Germany, given the utterly degrading conditions they had been subjected to. Their answer was: How could we leave? It would have meant giving up our homes, our work, our sources of income. Having been deprived by Nazi persecution and degradation of much of their self-respect, they had become unable to give up what still gave them a semblance of it: their earthly belongings. But instead of using possessions, they became captivated by them, and this possession by earthly goods became the fatal mask for their possession by anxiety, fear, and denial.

How the investment of personal property with one's life energy could make people die bit by bit was illustrated throughout the Nazi persecution of the Jews. At the time of the first boycott of Jewish stores, the chief external goal of the Nazis was to acquire the possessions of the Jews. They even let Jews take some things out of the country at that time if they would leave the bulk of their property behind. For a long time the intention of the Nazis, and the goal of their first discriminatory laws, was to force undesirable minorities, including Jews, into emigration.

Although the extermination policy was in line with the inner logic of Nazi racial ideology, one may wonder whether the idea that millions of Jews (and other foreign nationals) could be submitted to extermination did not partially result from seeing the degree of degradation Jews accepted without fighting back. When no violent resistance occurred, persecution of the Jews worsened, slow step by slow step.

Many Jews who on the invasion of Poland were able to survey their situation and draw the right conclusions survived the Second World War. As the Germans approached, they left everything behind and fled to Russia, much as they distrusted and disliked the Soviet system. But there, while badly treated, they could at least survive. Those who stayed on in Poland believing they could go on with life-as-before sealed their fate. Thus in the deepest sense the walk to the gas chamber was only the last consequence of these Jews' inability to comprehend what was in store; it was the final step of surrender to the death instinct, which might also be called the principle of inertia. The first step was taken long before arrival at the death camp.

We can find a dramatic demonstration of how far the surrender to inertia can be carried, and the wish not to know because knowing would create unbearable anxiety, in an experience of Olga Lengyel. She reports that although she and her fellow prisoners lived just a few hundred yards from the crematoria and the gas chambers and knew what they were for most prisoners denied knowledge of them for months. If they had grasped their true situation, it might have helped them save either the lives they themselves were fated to lose, or the lives of others.

When Mrs. Lengyel's fellow prisoners were selected to be sent to the gas chambers, they did not try to break away from the group, as she successfully did. Worse, the first time she tried to escape the gas chambers, some of the other selected prisoners told the supervisors that she was trying to get away. Mrs. Lengyel desperately asks the question: How was it possible that people denied the existence of the gas chambers when all day long they saw the crematoria burning and smelled the odor of burning flesh? Why did they prefer ignoring the exterminations to fighting for their very own lives? She can offer no explanation, only the observation that they resented anyone who tried to save himself from the common fate, because they lacked enough courage to risk action themselves. I believe they did it because they had given up their will to live and permitted their death tendencies to engulf them. As a result, such prisoners were in the thrall of the murdering SS not only physically but also psychologically, while this was not true for those prisoners who still had a grip on life.

Some prisoners even began to serve their executioners, to help speed the death of their own kind. Then things had progressed beyond simple inertia to the death instinct run rampant. Those who tried to serve their executioners in what were once their civilian capacities were merely continuing life as usual and therby opening the door to their death.

For example, Mrs. Lengyel speaks of Dr. Mengele, SS physician at Auschwitz, as a typical example of the "business as usual" attitude that enabled some prisoners, and certainly the SS, to retain whatever balance they could despite what they were doing. She describes how Dr. Mengele took all correct medical precautions during childbirth, rigorously observing all aseptic principles, cutting the umbilical cord with greatest care, etc. But only half an hour later he sent mother and infant to be burned in the crematorium.

Having made his choice, Dr. Mengele and others like him had to delude themselves to be able to live with themselves and their experience. Only one personal document on the subject has come to my attention, that of Dr. Nyiszli, a prisoner serving as "research physician" at Auschwitz. How Dr. Nyiszli deluded himself can be seen, for example, in the way he repeatedly refers to himself as working in Auschwitz as a physician, although he

worked as the assistant of a criminal murderer. He speaks of the Institute for
Race, Biological, and Anthropological Investigation as "one of the most
qualified medical centers of the Third Reich," although it was devoted to
proving falsehoods. That Nyiszli was a doctor didn't alter the fact that he—
like any of the prisoner foremen who served the SS better than some SS were
willing to serve it—was a participant in the crimes of the SS. How could he
do it and live with himself?

The answer is: by taking pride in his professional skills, irrespective of
the purpose they served. Dr. Nyiszli and Dr. Mengele were only two among
hundreds of other—and far more prominent—physicians who participated in
the Nazis' murderous pseudo-scientific human experiments. It was the peculiar pride of these men in their professional skill and knowledge, without
regard for moral implications, that made them so dangerous. Although the
concentration camps and crematoria are no longer here, this kind of pride
still remains with us; it is characteristic of a modern society in which fascination with technical competence has dulled concern for human feelings.
Auschwitz is gone, but so long as this attitude persists, we shall not be safe
from cruel indifference to life at the core.

I have met many Jews as well as gentile anti-Nazis, similar to the
activist group in Hungary described earlier, who survived in Nazi Germany
and in the occupied countries. These people realized that when a world goes
to pieces and inhumanity reigns supreme, man cannot go on living his
private life as he was wont to do, and would like to do; he cannot, as the
loving head of a family, keep the family living together peacefully, undisturbed by the surrounding world; nor can he continue to take pride in his
profession or possessions, when either will deprive him of his humanity, if
not also of his life. In such times, one must radically reevaluate all of what
one has done, believed in, and stood for in order to know how to act. In
short, one has to take a stand on the new reality—a firm stand, not one of
retirement into an even more private world.

If today, Negroes in Africa march against the guns of a police that
defends *apartheid*—even if hundreds of dissenters are shot down and tens of
thousands rounded up in camps—their fight will sooner or later assure them
of a chance for liberty and equality. Millions of the Jews of Europe who did
not or could not escape in time or go underground as many thousands did,
could at least have died fighting as some did in the Warsaw ghetto at the end,
instead of passively waiting to be rounded up for their own extermination.

LAWRENCE L. LANGER

The Americanization of the Holocaust
on Stage and Screen

We bring to the imaginative experience of the Holocaust a foreknowledge of man's doom. Not his fate, but his doom. The Greeks sat spellbound in their arenas in Athens and witnessed the unfolding of what they already knew: proud and defiant men and women submitting to an insurrection in their spirit that rebelled against limitations. Oedipus and Phaedra, Orestes and Antigone hurl their own natures against laws human or divine, suffer the intrusions of chance and coincidence, but *make their fate* by pursuing or being driven by weaknesses or strengths that are expressions of the human will. Whether they survive or die, they affirm the painful, exultant feeling of being human; they declare that man, in the moral world at least, is an agent in the fate we call his death.

But the doom we call extermination is another matter. The Athenians could identify the death of their heroes on the stage with a ritual for renewal, ally tragedy with comedy, and make both a cause for celebration. The human drama allowed it. But the Holocaust presents us with the spectacle of an inhuman drama: we sit in the audience and witness the unfolding of what we will never "know," even though the tales are already history. The tradition of fate encourages identification: we may not achieve the stature of an Oedipus or a Phaedra, but their problems of identify, of passion, of moral courage, or retribution, are human—are ours. The tradition of doom—a fate, one might

From *From Hester Street to Hollywood: The Jewish-American Stage and Screen.* © 1983 by Indiana University Press.

say, imposed on man by other men against his will, without his agency—
forbids identification: for who can share the last gasp of the victim of annihilation, whose innocence so totally dissevers him from his end? We lack the
psychological, emotional, and even intellectual powers to participate in a
ritual that celebrates *such* a demise. We feel alien, not akin. The drama of fate
reminds us that Man, should he so choose, can die for something; the drama
of doom, the history of the Holocaust, reveals that whether they chose or
not, men died for nothing.

This is not a comfortable theme for the artist to develop, or for an
audience to absorb. Traditions of heroic enterprise, in literature or in life;
conceptions of the human spirit, secular or divine; patterns for imagining
reality, whether written or oral—all have prepared us to view individual men
and women in a familiar way. Hence it should not be surprising that some of
the best known attempts to bring the Holocaust theme to the American stage
—Frances Goodrich and Albert Hackett's *The Diary of Anne Frank*, Millard
Lampell's *The Wall*, and Arthur Miller's *Incident at Vichy*—as well as films like
Judgment at Nuremberg and the TV "epic" *Holocaust*, should draw on old
forms to reassert man's fate instead of new ones to help us appreciate his
doom. To be sure, visually we have progressed in thirty years from the
moderate misery of a little room in Amsterdam to execution pits and peep-
holes into the gas chambers of Auschwitz in *Holocaust*; but imaginatively,
most of these works still cling valiantly to the illusion that the Nazi genocide
of nearly eleven million human beings has not substantially altered our vision
of human dignity. When Conrad's Marlow in *Heart of Darkness* returns from
the Congo to speak with Kurtz's Intended, he brings a message about Kurtz's
inhuman doom to a woman who wishes only to hear about his human fate.
And Marlow submits: the truth "would have been too dark—too dark altogether. . . . "

How much darkness must we acknowledge before we will be able to
confess that the Holocaust story cannot be told in terms of heroic dignity,
moral courage, and the triumph of the human spirit in adversity? Those
words adhere like burrs to the back of a patient beast, who lacks the energy
or desire to flick them away lest in doing so he disturb his tranquillity. Kurtz's
Intended pleads with Marlow for "something—something—to—live—
with." The Holocaust—alas!—provides us only with something to die with,
something from those who died with nothing left to give. There is no final
solace, no redeeming truth, no hope that so many millions may not have died
in vain. They have. But the American vision of the Holocaust, in the works
under consideration here, continues to insist that they have not, trying to
parlay hope, sacrifice, justice, and the future into a victory that will mitigate
despair. Perhaps it is characteristically American, perhaps merely human, but

these works share a deafness (in varying degrees) to those other words that Conrad's Marlow brings back only to find that he has no audience prepared to listen: " 'Don't you hear them?' The dusk was repeating them in a persistent whisper all around us, in a whisper that seemed to swell menacingly like the first whisper of a rising wind. 'The horror! The horror!'"

There is little horror in the stage version of *The Diary of Anne Frank:* there is very little in the original *Diary* itself. Perhaps this is one source of their appeal: they permit the imagination to cope with the idea of the Holocaust without forcing a confrontation with its grim details. Like the *Diary,* the play (though even more so) gives us only the bearable part of the story of Anne and the other occupants of the secret annex; the unbearable part begins after the final curtain falls and ends in Auschwitz and Bergen-Belsen. An audience coming to this play in 1955, only a decade after the event, would find little to threaten their psychological or emotional security. No one dies, and the inhabitants of the annex endure minimal suffering. The play really celebrates the struggle for harmony in the midst of impending disruption, thus supporting those values which the viewer instinctively hopes to find affirmed on the stage. To be sure, in the *Diary,* Anne is not oblivious to the doom of the Jews, despite her limited access to information; but there is no hint in the play of this entry from October 1942: "If it is as bad as this in Holland whatever will it be like in the distant and barbarous regions [the Jews] are sent to? We assume that most of them are murdered. The English radio speaks of their being gassed." In the *Diary,* however, Anne does not brood on the prospects of annihilation; she devotes most of her reflections to her aspirations as a writer and her passage through adolescence and puberty to young womanhood. Nevertheless, a certain amount of ambiguity lingers in her young mind (absent from her character in the play) that at least adds some complexity to her youthful vision. "I see the world being turned into a wilderness," she writes, "I hear the ever approaching thunder, which will destroy us too, I can feel the sufferings of millions and yet, if I look up into the heavens, I think that it will all come right, that this cruelty too will end, and that peace and tranquillity will return again." But for all but one of the inhabitants of the annex, nothing came right, cruelty grew worse, and neither peace nor tranquillity ever returned.

Yet this is not the feeling we are left with in the play, that accents Anne's mercurial optimism at the expense of the encroaching doom, which finally engulfed them all. Upbeat endings seem to be *de riguer* for the American imagination, which traditionally buries its tragedies and lets them fester in the shadow of forgetfulness. The drama begins with Mr. Frank, a "bitter old man," returning to the secret annex after the war and finding that Anne's diary has been preserved. His "reading" of excerpts becomes the substance of the play, which after the discovery and arrest fades back into the present, revealing a calm Mr. Frank, his bitterness gone. Considering the numerous "last glimpses" of Anne we might have received from this epilogue—one eyewitness in Bergen-Belsen, where she died, described her like this: "She was in rags. I saw her emaciated, sunken face in the darkness. Her eyes were very large"—one wonders at the stubborn, almost perverse insistence in the play on an affirmative epigraph, almost a denial of Anne's doom. Why should the authors think it important that we hear from Mr. Frank, in almost the last words of the play, the following tribute, *even if those words were quoted verbatim from Anne's real father*: "It seems strange to say this," muses Mr. Frank, "that anyone could be happy in a concentration camp. But Anne was happy in Holland where they first took us [i.e., Westerbork detention camp]."

The authors of the dramatic version of Anne Frank's *Diary* lacked the artistic will—or courage—to leave their audiences overwhelmed by the feeling that Anne's bright spirit was extinguished, that Anne, together with millions of others, was killed simply because she was Jewish, and for no other reason. This theme lurks on the play's periphery, but never emerges into the foreground, though one gets a vague hint during the *Hanukkah* celebration that ends Act One. That Anne herself, had she survived, would have been equal to this challenge is suggested by her brief description of a roundup of Amsterdam Jews witnessed from her attic window: "In the evenings when it's dark, I often see rows of good, innocent people accompanied by crying children, walking on and on, in charge of a couple of Germans, bullied and knocked about until they almost drop. No one is spared—old people, babies, expectant mothers, the sick—each and all join in the march of death." But the audience in the theater is sheltered from this somber vision, lest it disrupt the mood of carefully orchestrated faith in human nature that swells into a crescendo just before the play's climax, when the Gestapo and Green Police arrive to arrest the inhabitants of the annex. One is forced to contemplate Anne's restive intelligence at its most simple-minded, as Goodrich and Hackett have her reply to Peter Van Daan's irritable impatience at their dilemma with the pitiful cliché: "We're not the only people that've had to suffer. There've always been people that've had to. . . . " Anne's mind was more capacious, if still undeveloped, but a probe into the darker realms that Conrad and Marlow knew of, an entry like the following from Anne's *Diary*, would have introduced a discordant note into the crescendo I have mentioned: "There's in people simply an urge to destroy, an urge to kill, to murder and rage, and until all mankind, without exception, undergoes a great change, wars will be waged, everything that has been built up, cultivated, and grown will be destroyed and disfigured, after which mankind will have to begin all over again."

This view of the apocalypse before any fresh resurrection appears nowhere in the stage version of Anne's *Diary*. Indeed, its presence in the other works I will examine will be one test of their authenticity as Holocaust literature. If in the end even Anne Frank retreated to a safer cheerfulness, we need to remember that she was not yet fifteen when she wrote that passage. The line that concludes her play, floating over the audience like a benediction assuring grace after momentary gloom, is the least appropriate epitaph conceivable for the millions of victims and thousands of survivors of Nazi genocide: "in spite of everything, I still believe that people are really good at heart." Those who permit such heartwarming terms to insulate them against the blood-chilling events they belie need to recall that they were written by a teenager who could also say of her situation: "I have often been downcast, but never in despair; I regard our hiding as a dangerous adventure, romantic and interesting at the same time." Her strong sentimental strain, which was only part of her nature, dominates the drama, and ultimately diverts the audience's attention from the sanguinary to the sanguine, causing them to forget that the roots are identical, and that during the Holocaust man's hope was stained by a blood more indelible than the imaginary spot so distressing to Lady Macbeth. By sparing us the imaginative ordeal of such consanguinity, the drama of *The Diary of Anne Frank* cannot begin to evoke the doom that eventually denied the annex's victims the dignity of human choice.

The play presents instead a drama of domestic pathos; it begins and ends with the figure of Mr. Frank, a *paterfamilias* without a family who nevertheless is inspired, like the rest of us, by his dead daughter's steadfast devotion to hope. Bruno Bettelheim's needlessly harsh criticism of the Frank family for failing to recognize the crisis for Jews in Europe and to increase the prospect of survival by seeking separate hiding places, nevertheless implies an important truth for anyone seeking to portray the Holocaust experience with insight. The family unit, that traditional bulwark in moments of familiar stress, was worthless and occasionally injurious to individual survival in the unpredictable atmosphere of the deathcamp. The tensions that sundered such ancient loyalties are absent from *Anne Frank*; they begin to appear in Millard Lampell's play *The Wall* (1960), based on John Hersey's novel, but even here, under the pressures of life in the Warsaw Ghetto, family unity finally asserts itself and triumphs over the strains that threaten to crack it.

The American imagination seems reluctant to take the non-Kierkegaardian leap into unfaith that might reveal a vision like the following, from the Auschwitz stories, *This Way for the Gas, Ladies and Gentlemen*, of the Polish survivor Tadeusz Borowski:

Here is a woman—she walks quickly, but tries to appear calm. A small child with a pink cherub's face runs after her and, unable to keep up, stretches out his little arms and cries: "Mama! Mama!"

"Pick up your child, woman!"

"It's not mine, sir, not mine!" she shouts hysterically and runs on, covering her face with her hands. She wants to hide, she wants to reach those who will not ride the trucks, those who will go on foot, those who will stay alive. She is young, healthy, good-looking, she wants to live.

But the child runs after her, wailing loudly: "Mama, mama, don't leave me!"

"It's not mine, not mine, no!"

One has only to immerse oneself in this situation to understand how thoroughly the Nazi system of terror and genocide poisoned that vital source of human dignity, that made man an instrument in his fate: the phenomenon of choice. Mother and child is a comforting image when the mother can do something to comfort her child: but how does one comfort her child when both are on their way to the gas chamber? Futility drives the mother in this fictional passage—though we have eyewitness testimony to prove the historical bases of moments like these—to a repudiation unthinkable for the civilized mind. But Auschwitz introduced the realm of the unthinkable into the human drama, and no representation of the Holocaust that ignores this realm can be considered complete.

Lampell's *The Wall* peers into its dark recesses, but finally withdraws to reassert a familiar moral view. It is too dark—too dark altogether. "Man as a helpless victim," writes Lampell in his introduction to the play. "I do not deny that this is a truth of our time. But it is only one truth. There are others. There is understanding, and indomitable faith, and the rare, exultant moments when one human finally reaches out to accept another." But can one truth be severed from the other? And how do those rare exultant moments affect the doom of the eleven million helpless victims who did not survive to appreciate them? Lampell chose to avoid this question by searching for flickering rays amid the brooding gloom. His initial response to the plan to dramatize the Hersey novel was to immerse himself in documents and writings about the Warsaw Ghetto. When he discovered—to his dismay—that "what was unique in Warsaw was the scope of man's inhumanity to man," he was reduced to "an overwhelming sense of ashes and agony" and almost abandoned the project. His reason would be ludicrous, were the subject not so grave: "I am a writer chiefly concerned with life, not death." By temporarily retreating in despair from the ruins of the Ghetto because "I simply could not recognize human life as I knew it," Lampell unwittingly refused the higher challenge of the Holocaust experience—its utter transformation of human life as we know it. By finally accepting the "lower challenge" and building his play about the safer theme of men "in spite of it all, stumbling toward a possible dignity," he still writes an honest play, better theater than *The Diary of Anne Frank*, but one not governed by the inner momentum of the Holocaust toward extermination. Instead, Lampell restores to men an instrumentality in their fate; a handful of Jews, he insists, "exposed the fullest potential of the human race." Whether this is solace for the 300,000 other Jews of the Ghetto who were deported to Treblinka (not Auschwitz, as the play suggests) and murdered, Lampell does not consider; but the impact of the dramatic spectacle is to affirm the heroic fate of the few, and to mute the unmanageable doom of the wretched rest.

The consolation of the *Hanukkah* celebration at the midpoint of *The Diary of Anne Frank* has its analogue at the exact midpoint of *The Wall*: the wedding of Mordecai and Rutka. But Lampell has established an effective tension between joy and terror, for while the wedding ceremony proceeds indoors, the first roundups of Jews for deportation to "labor camps" occur in the streets outside. The counterpoint between the grave Chassidic dance of Reb Mazur and the confused screams of terrified Jews fleeing for their lives in disorder, between the lively *hora* of the celebrants and the thudding boots of the Nazis, defines two alienated realms—and suggests the futility of the Jews' trying to inhabit both. Bruno Bettelheim had charged that the Franks' refusal to abandon family ritual and tradition had cost them their lives, though he seemed unable to admit that after twenty-five months of security in their haven, with the Allies moving on Paris and soon to be in Belgium, the Franks had sufficient reason to believe that their strategy for survival would work. Lampell assumes a more complex view, acknowledging how insidiously the Nazi threat of extermination could infiltrate the family unit itself. The desperate dependence on stability represents almost willful blindness on the part of the Ghetto inhabitants, and to his credit, Lampell makes this "refusal to see" the dramatic focus of the second half of the play.

What it amounts to, for the historic individual as well as the dramatic character, for the artist, the reader, and the audience, is accepting the credibility of doom (extermination in the gas chamber for being a Jew) when all our lives we have struggled to absorb the painful truth of our mortality, "merely" the necessity for our death—man's fate. Against that fate we can mount consolations, and even some forms of transcendence—faith, love, children, creative endeavor, some communion with the future that liberates us from the prison of our mortality. But what promised to free the human spirit from the deathcamp, the gas chamber, and the crematorium? This is the question to which Lampell is committed—*before* the act of creation—to finding an affirmative answer. Such commitment requires him to manipulate probability and distort the balance between heroism and despair, as if a prior espousal of human community, even amidst the rubble of the destroyed Ghetto, were the only way to make the Holocaust acceptable on the stage. To be sure, violations of that sense of community appear in the play. The *paterfamilias* here, Pan Apt, the father of Rachel, Halinka, David, and Mordecai, repudiates his Jewish heritage and with forged papers flees to the Polish side of the Wall, deserting his family. Stefan, Reb Mazur's son, joins the Jewish Ghetto police because of the Nazi promise that he and his family will be safe from deportations. But in order to save himself, he is reduced to pleading with his own father to consent to "resettlement." Nazi doom left the individual no simple way of surviving with dignity: one had to pay a human price for his life, and in *The Wall*, that price is usually a disruption of family integrity. The one place where such integrity *is* preserved is one of the least probable (though most reassuring) moments of the play, infringing on the authenticity of history and of human doom in the Holocaust. Huddled in their bunker as Nazi troops are rooting out the scattered remnants of resis- tance, Mordecai, Rutka, their baby (born in the Ghetto) and a few other underground fighters are about to make their way through the sewers to safety outside the Wall, when a detachment of German soldiers spots them. Withdrawing into the bunker again, they wait in silence, when suddenly the baby begins to cry. We have ample evidence of parents smothering their infants to protect themselves and often larger groups from detection, but Lampell flinches before this ultimate rejection of the family bond: it, too, would have been too dark—too dark altogether. His scene direction reads: "Mordecai puts his hand over the baby's mouth. Rutka stands it as long as she can, then shoves his hand away." The baby cries again, and of course the Germans hear him. Verisimilitude, human as well as aesthetic truth, would require the capture of the Jews at this point; instead, in an utterly uncon- vincing denouement, Berson leaves the bunker undetected and draws the soldiers away with the sound of his concertina. The heroic impulse triumphs over truth, Berson sacrifices himself that others may live (assuming they do: otherwise his gesture would be doubly futile), and man proves himself still in control of his fate, willing to surrender the life of a man in order to assure the continuity of the Life of Men.

One of the paradoxes of this play, and of much Holocaust literature, is that it tries to serve two masters. When Rachel reports to her horrified fellow Jews about evidence that the deported victims—men, women, and chil- dren—are not being resettled but murdered, they are unable to believe her. "It doesn't make sense," cries Reb Mazur. "All right, they're not civilized," objects Mordecai, her brother, "But they're still human." And the rabbi later affirms: "Yes, I am calm—because I know that any faith based on love and respect will outlive any faith based on murder." One "master" which this play serves is a familiar but weary vocabulary, words like "sense," "civilized," "human," "faith," "love," and "respect," which desperate men and women cling to, to shore up the ruins of their crumbling world. They lead finally to the heroic if ultimately futile resistance that concludes the play—futile because the Jews possess neither numbers nor weapons sufficient to defeat the Germans. The other "master," mouthed but not acted upon by the briefly cynical Berson, represents a subterranean truth of the Holocaust that art has not yet found an adequate vocabulary to explore: "Love. What does it mean? When they come with guns, I have seen a son beat his own mother. A mother throw her child out of the window, her own child that she bore inside her." We get a glimpse later on of the motive that leads Berson to a moral reversal, bringing him back into the Ghetto after he has left it: "I always thought that just to live was enough. To live *how*? To live *with whom*?" But fine sentiments cannot replace the searching psychological analyses art must provide us with if we are to understand how the human creature reacts when he realizes that his enemy is neither "civilized" nor "human," and when the reality threatening to consume him resembles nothing his mind or soul has ever faced before.

The handful of survivors of the Warsaw Ghetto left behind them a world destroyed, one that their lives could not redeem, their memories not revive. The Nazis did their work thoroughly. Nevertheless, like *The Diary of Anne Frank*, *The Wall* reverberates with its memorable line, its token of hope, its verbal gesture of affirmation: "the only way to answer death is with more life." And abstractly, conceptually, philosophically, it is a noble refrain: but whether Rachel will indeed survive to bear a child in defiance of all these atrocities, we will never know. An even more significant hiatus is the absence of some notion of how such new life "responds" to the multitudinous deaths of the Holocaust. The teasing hint that somehow the future will bring palliatives for such anguish deflects our attention from a harsher truth of the Holocaust, which the play flirts with only to retreat from: that sometimes, many times, the only way to answer your own possible death was with someone else's life. John Hersey, in one crucial episode in the novel at least, does not flinch from this harsher truth: when the baby begins to cry, an underground leader takes it from its mother's arms and smothers it. Doomed people do not behave like men and women in charge of their fate. Lampell was probably correct in assuming that his audience would not tolerate such agony: but *The Wall*, like all art, pays a price for such compromise.

Moral oversimplification is one of the many sins afflicting writing about the Holocaust. We find comfort in schemes of cause and effect: villains destroy, victims submit or resist. We will never understand the behavior of the victims until we gain greater insight into the motives of their murderers. The courageous fighters of the Warsaw Ghetto, too few and too late, with scant help from the Polish underground and virtually none from the world outside, knew in advance that they were not choosing life but exerting minimum control over the manner of their death, rescuing a fragment of fate from a seemingly unassailable doom. That doom is personified by their enemies, but in *The Wall* they are mechanized, dehumanized, transformed into robots called merely German Private, German Sergeant, and O.S. Fuehrer. They differ little from the loudspeaker attached to a linden tree, barking orders for assembly and "resettlement." But the Jews were killed by men and women like themselves, not by automatons: one of the play's major faults is its failure to confront the challenge of characterizing those instruments of doom who, through a combination of ruthlessness and manipulation, deprived their victims of moral space to maneuver with dignity.

Regardless of their artistic merit, the plays and films we are examining share one common purpose: they bring us into the presence of human beings searching for a discourse commensurate with their dilemma. In order to recognize that dilemma (the threat of extermination), they must find a language adequate to express it; but in order to find that language, they must first be able to imagine the dilemma. Without such perception, without the words to articulate it to others and make it credible, the individual remains totally vulnerable. Even *with* such "ammunition," after a certain point in time, the Jew had few meaningful alternatives (though many hopeless ones); those left with moral space to maneuver with dignity were the non-Jews, and to his credit Arthur Miller in *Incident at Vichy* (1964) shifts the center of moral responsibility for the situation of the Jews from the victims to the well-intentioned spectator, who begins by dismissing Nazism as "an outburst of vulgarity" but ends by realizing that a more precise definition must move him from language and perception to deeds—a process similar to the one followed by the Warsaw Ghetto fighters, though their decision to act could not support anyone's survival.

Except for a gypsy, all the characters in *Incident at Vichy* have been rounded up because they are suspected of being Jews. How is the Jew to protect himself against such danger, psychologically, without supporting his enemy's view of him as a menace to society? He was vulnerable precisely because he was *not* able to see himself in this way: "You begin wishing you'd committed a crime, you know? Something definite," says Lebeau, the painter, "I was walking down the street before, a car pulls up beside me, a man gets out and measures my nose, my ears, my mouth, the next thing I'm sitting in a police station—or whatever the hell this is here—and in the middle of Europe, the highest peak of civilization!" Kafka could impose on life the discontinuities of art and the courageous reader might follow his vision with impunity; but when life imposed on the Jews Kafkan discontinuities like the one Lebeau describes, the confused and terrorized victim could not retreat for insight or relief to the sanctuary of art. Indeed, *Incident at Vichy* may be seen as concisely dramatized dialogues between points of view which question the power of art—on the Holocaust theme—to achieve these ends. Insight and relief are allied to meaning, but when one of the prisoners mouths the cliché that one "should try to think of why things happen. It helps to know the meaning of one's suffering," the painter—recalling that he has been arrested and possibly doomed because of the size of his nose— acidly replies: "After the Romans and the Greeks and the Renaissance, and you know what this means?"

When humanistic precedents collapse, the individual loses the security of collective identity; neither family nor group nor profession protects: the prisoners in this play are isolated, alone, searching for private strategies to insure their release—unaware that the Nazi determination to destroy all Jews has deprived them of choice. The contest is unequal before it begins. If art is an illusion we submit to for greater insight, life—the life depicted in *Incident at Vichy*—is an illusion we submit to from greater ignorance. Habitual ways of thinking become parodies of insight; to rumors about Auschwitz the actor Monceau replies: "Is that really conceivable to you? War is War, but you still have to keep a certain sense of proportion. I mean Germans are still *people*." His naiveté about the equivalence of words to facts breeds futile hopes. Incapable of suspecting that the Germans will identify Jews by ordering them to drop their trousers, he urges his fellow prisoners not to look like victims: "One must create one's own reality in this world. . . . One must show them the face of a man who is right." Unlike the authors of *Anne Frank* and *The Wall*, Miller has the artistic integrity to expose the impotence of such facile rhetoric. Even more irrelevant is the electrician Bayard's conviction that one must not respond personally to the Nazi threat: they may torture the individual, but "they can't torture the future." Only Von Berg, the non-Jew "spectator" who knows that he can secure release by identifying himself, moves toward a clear perception of the future: "What if nothing comes of the facts but endless, endless disaster?"

Miller has a lucid sense of the impotence of the Jewish victims, once they have lost the flexibility of their freedom. They talk of overpowering the solitary guard and fleeing, but a combination of fear, uncertainty, and lack of weapons frustrates this plan, especially after a sympathetic major warns them that armed guards stand outside. They berate themselves for not having been more wary *before* their arrest. But as Von Berg implies, decent men do not possess an imagination for disaster, especially one ending in gas chamber and oven. This is the source of Nazi strength, he argues: they do the inconceivable, and "it paralyzes the rest of us." The consequences for values, for human behavior, are alarming, if not revolutionary: "You must not calculate these people with some nineteenth-century arithmetic of loss and gain . . . in my opinion, win or lose this war, they have pointed the way to the future. What one used to conceive a human being to be will have no room on this earth." One would like to believe that this is merely the language of fashionable despair, coming from an Austrian aristocrat who can still describe the Nazi menace as "the nobility of the totally vulgar." The doctor Leduc, Prince Von Berg's chief disputant and interlocutor as the others "disappear" into the inner office, refines the Austrian's observation by describing how the Nazis capitalize on their victims' habit of projecting their own reasonable ideas— like the impossibility of extermination—into their enemy's head. "Do you understand?" he pleads. "You cannot wager your life on a purely rational analysis of this situation."

As they wait in this anteroom to deportation and death wears on, façades begin to fall away, and certain truths emerge which, if organized into a system of belief, would indeed transform our vision of what it was like to have been alive in that time—to say nothing of our own. Miller provides insight into the psychology—not necessarily of the Jew—but of the *hunted*, the humiliated, the disenfranchised, the abandoned, the scorned. Lebeau the painter admits to believing in the disaster that threatens, and to exposing himself to danger nonetheless: "you get tired of believing in the truth. You get tired of seeing things clearly." To perceive with the illogic of the Nazis, to endorse, for example, the impossibility of being a Jew in Hitler's Europe, was to accept the erosion of one's own humanity. Unwilling to embrace this course, *unable* to do so in the absence of model precedents, the victim was driven through sheer moral weariness to accept his own mortality, his vulnerability: "one way or the other," says the doctor, "with illusions or without them, exhausted or fresh—we have been trained to die. The Jew and the Gentile both."

But even this seemingly final view is only one in a series of carefully orchestrated positions in *Incident at Vichy*: until the play's last moment, Miller withholds the heroic gesture that we have encountered in *Anne Frank* and *The Wall*, and which even he cannot ultimately resist, though he shrouds it with some ambiguity. Holocaust writing itself serves two masters: a clear intellectual perception of how Nazism shrank the area of dignified choice and reduced the options for human gestures; and the instinct to have victims survive heroically even within these less-than-human alternatives. When the German Major (who has been struggling, as a military man, against his own association with the S.S. inquisitor) asks Leduc whether he would refuse, if he were released and the others kept, the doctor murmurs "No"; and to the more complex (and deliberately nastier) question of whether he would walk out of the door with a light heart, he can only reply: "I don't know." The confrontation is a *locus classicus* for understanding how the Holocaust undermined what Von Berg would have called the "nineteenth-century arithmetic of loss and gain"—or right and wrong. "One man's death is another man's bread" ran a bitter slogan in the deathcamps, and it represents a far deeper and more painful truth than the principle that in spite of everything, men are really good at heart, or that the only way to answer death is with more life.

In the end, Miller concedes, perception changes little: the non-Jew will live not because he is a better man, but because he is not Jewish; the Jew will die, simply because he is Jewish. Such "logic" fits no moral scheme, generates no satisfactory mode of behavior. Viable attitudes may strengthen the moral will, but only viable acts save the physical self. Miller discovers such an act to end his play—Von Berg gives his pass to Leduc, allowing the Jewish doctor to walk safely past the guard while he himself remains behind to face the wrath of the Nazis—but the gesture simply imposes on a hopeless situation the temporary idealism of self-sacrifice. Von Berg has learned how to share the anguish of the Jew, to cross the terrain separating the complicity of silence from the helplessness of the victim. But as the curtain descends, more men rounded up as suspected Jews appear. One can hardly believe that Leduc will get far with the police in close pursuit, and the routine of identification and deportation is about to begin again.

The motive for Von Berg's gesture is left in doubt: has he tried to save another man, or his own soul? At least he has acknowledged a vital truth of the Holocaust: to be alive while others perish innocently in the gas chambers is itself a form of complicity. The Jew, as Leduc insists, has learned a grim lesson about the nature of man: "that he is *not* reasonable, that he is full of murder, that his ideals are only the little tax he pays for the right to hate and kill with a clear conscience." *He* has seen into the heart of darkness.

Despite his lucidity about the "vulgar" Nazis, Von Berg clings to his ancient idealism, as the only prop that still supports his flagging life: "There are people who would find it easier to die than stain one finger with this murder." One might interpret this dialogue as a confrontation between the voice of a doomed man and one who still believes that he can master his own fate. But the irony of the moment is Von Berg's slow realization that he can restore the challenge of fate to Leduc only by surrendering his own, and submitting to the doom that the Jew now hopes to escape. One would feel more elated about this tribute to the human spirit were it not surrounded by the disappearance of the other Jews and the arrival of new victims who will have no one to "save" them. Von Berg has repudiated the idea of man's right to hate and kill with a clear conscience. A world without ideals, as he said earlier, would be intolerable. But how does one measure his private deed of generosity against the slaughter of millions? Does it invalidate Leduc's melancholy charge, only too familiar to survivors of the deathcamps, that "Each man has his Jew . . . the man whose death leaves you relieved that you are not him, despite your decency?" Miller at least pays homage to the ambiguity of efforts to redress the imbalance between justice and suffering imposed by the Nazi atrocities. But the magnitude of the sorrow and loss dwarfs the deed, however noble, of one man for one man; *Incident at Vichy* illuminates the difficulty, perhaps the impossibility, of affirming the tragic dignity of the individual man, when it has been soiled by the ashes of anonymous millions.

If *Incident at Vichy* exposes the dilemma of measuring the private deed of generosity against the slaughter of millions, Abby Mann's script for the Stanley Kramer production of *Judgement at Nuremberg* (1961) raises the issue of measuring the public act of justice against the same slaughter. If Miller's play complicates the problem of redressing the imbalance between justice and such suffering, Kramer's film simplifies the question of establishing a connection between mass atrocity and individual responsibility. The force of idealism in *Judgement at Nuremberg* resides not in the faith of a young girl, or a beleaguered Ghetto fighter, or an Austrian aristocrat, but in a principle: that in a court of law, with only relevant testimony allowed, where defendants have counsel who may cross-examine witnesses, a just verdict against an unjust act somehow satisfies the conscience even though political expediency—in this instance, the Berlin Airlift and its consequences for German-American relations—may afterwards undermine its durability. Just before the final fadeout, the audience is treated to the unsavory irony that by July 14, 1949, after the last of the so-called second Nuremberg trials, of "ninety-nine sentenced to prison terms, not one is still serving his sentence."

I suppose that for those who still see the Holocaust as a situation of violated justice, this announcement is as exasperating and offensive as the news in 1980 that 200 alleged Nazi war criminals are still living safely in the United States. But both truths are accompanied by an overwhelming sense of futility, especially to those who have already understood that the logic of law can never make sense of the illogic of extermination. The film tries to do exactly the reverse; how else are we to interpret its final episode, with its unqualified assumption that the perversion of justice necessarily leads to genocide? The trial over, the guilty verdicts in, the life sentences proclaimed, the Chief Judge Dan Haywood (Spencer Tracy) confronts the chief defendant, former Nazi Minister of Justice Ernst Janning (Burt Lancaster), who "doomed" himself in court by honorably announcing that "if there is to be any salvation for Germany those of us who know our guilt must admit it no matter what the cost in pain and humiliation." The two representatives of justice, now and then, face each other, and Janning says to Haywood: "I want to hear from a man like you. A man who has heard what happened. I want to hear—not that he forgives—but that he understands." The kind of insight (if not charity) demanded by this question, the film does not know how to dramatize. Whether because of a failure of nerve, of dramatic sense, or of artistic imagination, the author and director have not solved the problem of exploring this difficult psychological issue in their courtroom drama. Judge Haywood gropes for a response in a scene direction in the script, but this is conveyed to the audience only through the inarticulate furrows of Spencer Tracy's brow: "understand," Haywood says to himself. "I understand the pressures you were under. . . . But how can I understand the deaths of millions of men, women, and children in gas ovens [a common technical blunder fusing and confusing gas chambers with crematorium ovens], Herr Janning?" A shrewd interpreter of furrowed brows, Janning replies in stereotypical and (as we shall see) self-contradictory justification: "I did not know it would come to that. You must believe it. You must believe it." The judge's rejoinder is the closing line of the film: "Herr Janning. It came to that the first time you sentenced a man to death you knew to be innocent." A melodramatic riposte, precise and compact: but are we expected to be content with this explanation of the murder of six million Jews and five million other innocent human beings? When decent men, thought tacit or active consent, from personal gain, weak will, or false patriotism, authorize (as in this film) the sterilization of a Communist's son or the execution of an elderly Jew on the trumped-up charge of cohabiting with an Aryan, they participate in a totalitarian manipulation of the law against certain individuals—but do they lay the groundwork for the annihilation of a people?

That annihilation is central to the historical truth behind the film, if not to its artistic logic: no serious treatment of the Holocaust can avoid it. But *Judgement at Nuremberg* introduces evidence about Buchenwald and Belsen in an almost gratuitous fashion, though the impact of these actual Army films on cast and audience is unquestionable; indeed, instead of establishing continuity between the horrifying events and the deeds of the defendants, the images of atrocity on a screen within a screen create a psychological distance: what system of justice can render homage to the mounds of corpses being shoved into a mass grave by a giant British bulldozer? The real event of atrocity and the subsequent film using it as a background do not cohere in a satisfying image of deed and consequence, uniting the twisted bodies of the victims with the acts of the four men on trial. At the end, Janning protests "I did not know it would come to that." But earlier, during his moment of "confession," he is more precise: "Maybe we didn't know the details. But if we didn't know, it was because we didn't want to know." The space between these two statements, between denial and equivocation, forms a psychological desert that the film doesn't begin to explore. Yet that wasteland is exactly the area whose detailed examination would make a film like *Judgment at Nuremberg* worthy of our attention. Three of the four German judges on trial are puppets in the dock, masks of contempt, indifference, or apprehension, but never human beings. The unrepentant Nazi, the timid collaborator, and the perennial self-justifier are familiar stereotypical figures whose presence in the film offer no insight whatsoever into the nature of the genocidal impulse. And Ernst Janning doesn't help us by denouncing himself as worse than any of them "because he knew what they were and went along with them." Nor does his self-portrait, shaded with aristocratic disdain—he "made his life . . . excrement because he walked with them"—suggest any of the moral chiaroscuro that might fall from the master hand of a Rembrandt. Janning's declaration of guilt is not enough, psychologically or artistically: not enough for himself, because he still has not penetrated his motives, and not enough for us, because we still do not know how such a decent man came to lend his judicial prestige to the Nazi cause.

Admission of guilt neither restores decency—the lingering horrors of Belsen insure this in the film—nor explains its perversion, any more than Albert Speer's acknowledgement (at the primary Nuremberg trial and in his memoirs) of responsibility for Nazi crimes he claims to have known nothing about restores our faith in him or explains the tangled motives that led him to embrace the aspirations of the Third Reich. Nor does the eloquent speech of Rolfe the defense attorney, ably portrayed by Maximilian Schell, take us any deeper into the heart of Holocaust darkness. By expanding the perimeters of guilt—"The whole world is as responsible for Hitler as is Germany"—Rolfe seeks to mitigate blame for his client; but under the burden of eleven million innocent victims, the structure of this argument collapses too. Although the immediate thrust of the film is to leave the audience feeling the irony of the conflict between political expediency and absolute justice, the perhaps unintended momentum of its subterranean current—reinforced by the impact of the documentary views of the camp—is to oppress the audience with the irrelevance of absolute justice to the collective crime of mass murder. In the aftermath of such "indecent" dying, the courtroom as *mise en scéne* for a comprehension of its enormity seems pitifully inadequate. Like most Hollywood efforts, this admittedly serious film scants the more complex interior landscape of the mind, where Judge, Victim, and Accused surrender the clear outlines of their identity and wrestle with a reality that subverts the very meaning of decency. *Judgement at Nuremberg*, with its concluding irony that by July 1949 none of the 99 sentenced to prison at the last of the second series of trials was still behind bars, renders a *Judgment of Nuremberg*, of Nazism, and of the contemporary world that it probably never wished to impose: that uncorrupted justice, the highest expression of law, order, morality, and civilization, is only a charade in the presence of atrocities literally embodied by the mounds of twisted corpses in mass graves at Belsen. The film uses the Holocaust theme only to misuse it; it focuses momentarily on the original horror, then shifts our awareness (thereby once more warming our hearts) to the admirable probity of an amiable American judge. If the irony of history allying Germany with one former enemy against another former one, has the last word, what happens to the responsibility of art, which must avoid the trivialization of that horror despite history's insensitivity? This is the real weakness of *Judgement at Nuremberg*, which mirrors that insensitivity while pretending that the temporary triumph of justice over expediency—German or American—can make a difference.

"To produce a mighty book," Melville says in *Moby Dick*, "you must choose a mighty theme." Perhaps modesty kept him from adding that a mighty talent was also necessary. Few contemporary themes present "mightier" challenges to the imagination than the Holocaust, the implacable, mesmerizing White Whale of our time; but when American television committed millions to produce Gerald Green's documentary drama, *Holocaust*, those who provided the money did not suspect that they had invested in a dolphin, though having been promised a whale. Had the makers of this mammoth enterprise been more attuned to sacred scripture, they might have been forewarned of the danger of trying to draw out leviathan with a hook.

When a famous survivor of Auschwitz, Elie Wiesel, protested in print that, whatever its intentions, *Holocaust* "transforms an ontological event into soap-opera," Green defended himself by citing the contrary views of distinguished critics like John Rich, Tom Shales, and Harriet Van Horne. To justify himself against the charge of large-scale mingling of fiction with historical fact, he cited the earlier example of *War and Peace*, compounding his sponsor's mistake of confusing dolphins with whales. The real issue was lucidly raised by *Time* writer Lance Morrow: "one senses something wrong with the television effort when one realizes that two or three black-and-white concentration-camp still photographs displayed by Dorf [fictional SS officer]—the stacked, starved bodies—are more powerful and heartbreaking than two or three hours of dramatization." Morrow goes on to complain that the "last 15 minutes of Vittorio De Sica's *The Garden of the Finzi-Continis*, in which Italian Jews are rounded up to be taken to the camps, is more wrenching than all the hours of *Holocaust*"—a judgment with which I happen to agree. At least two crucial issues are raised here, both of which need to be addressed before anyone can respond intelligently to the television drama *Holocaust*.

The first is the question of whether that "ontological event" *can* be transformed into a form of artistic experience carrying it beyond its historical moment and making it accessible in all its complexity to those who have not directly experienced it. Can representation rival the immediacy of contemporaneous photographs, diaries dug up after the war in the ashes surrounding Auschwitz, or even survivor accounts—unromantic emotions recollected in disquietude? Nothing can rival the chaotic masses of undifferentiated corpses, the token of men's doom in the Holocaust; but I would suggest that only art can lead the uninitiated imagination from the familiar realm of man's fate to the icy atmosphere of the deathcamps, where collective doom replaced the private will. Holocaust art is transitional art, a balloon, as it were, straining to break free from its inspiring reality but always moored by a single stubborn strand to the ontological event that gave it birth—the extermination of millions of innocent human beings. It is a necessary art, ever more necessary as that even recedes in time and new generations struggle to comprehend why a civilized country in the midst of the twentieth century coolly decided to murder all of Europe's Jews. The documents themselves do not answer this vital question for us.

Does television's *Holocaust*? Many who celebrate the film argue that for the first time, at least in America, viewers will get a sense of what it was like to suffer being Jewish during the Nazi period. Nothing before on American stage or screen had faced so "fearlessly" the fact of genocide, and the process which led up to it. The uninitiated imagination is offered Kristallnacht, the euthanasia program, the Warsaw Ghetto, Buchenwald, Theresienstadt, Auschwitz, Sobibor, and Babi Yar—to say nothing of Eichmann, Heydrich, Ohlendorf, Biberstein, Blobel and several others in the hierarchy of Nazi executioners. One sees Jews being beaten, starved, tortured, marching primly into the gas chambers of Auschwitz, tumbling docilely into the murder pits at Babi Yar. One hears Erik Dorf and his historical counterparts speaking of Jews as if they were vermin, superfluous equipment, detritus on the shores of Europe. Why is it then that even Kurtz's Intended might have watched this spectacle without feeling that it was too dark—too dark altogether? Why is it that nothing in the drama equals or even approaches the unmitigated horror of the actual films of Nazi executions which Dorf shows his superiors? One might argue that art never matches history; but in the case of *Holocaust*, it is more valid to conclude that talent has not matched intention. The failure of *Holocaust* is a failure of imagination. The vision which plunges us into the lower abysses of atrocity is not there. We do not know what it was like, in the

Warsaw Ghetto and elsewhere, to have been reduced to eating dogs, cats, horses, insects, and even, in rare unpublicized instances, human flesh. We do not know what the human being suffered during days and nights in sealed boxcars, starving, confused, desperate, sharing one's crowded space with frozen corpses. We do not know of the endless rollcalls in Auschwitz, often in sub-freezing temperature, when men and women simply collapsed and died from exhaustion. We have abundant examples of husbands and wives clinging together in adverse conditions, but we never glimpse—as I mentioned earlier—mothers abandoning children or fathers and sons throttling each other for a piece of bread. We see well-groomed and sanitized men and women filing into the gas chamber, but what does this convey of the terror and despair that overwhelmed millions of victims as they recognized the final moment of their degradation and their powerlessness to respond? Perhaps art will never be able to duplicate the absolute horror of such atrocities: but if it cannot recreate at least a limited authentic image of that horror—and *Holocaust* does not—then audiences will remain as deceived about the *worst* as young Anne Frank's lingering words on the essential good ness of human nature deceive us about the *best*.

A second crucial test of all Holocaust art is the question of insight. Having viewed *Holocaust*, do we have any *fresh* insights into the Nazi mind, the victim, the spectator? The drama chooses the least arduous creative path, tamely following chronological sequence, though the disruption of time-sense (and place-sense) was one of the chief features of the deathcamp experience: tomorrow vanished, and the past became a dim, nostalgic echo. It adopts the safe strategy of externalizing the event. A doctor sends Anna Weiss to Hadamar, notorious euthanasia center in prewar Germany, but neither he, nor her sister-in-law (who consents to let her go), nor the nurses who receive her, nor the group of puppet-like figures who join her in the walk to their death, reveal any vivid anguish, any searing conflict, any terror, pain or even dislocation of the moral center of their being. If extermination *is* such a simple matter of banality (and I do not believe it), it is hardly worth writing about. Even more impoverished (in terms of fresh insight) is the spectacle of Dr. Weiss and his friend Lowy lamely walking to their doom in the gas chambers of Auschwitz. What do men think or feel at that moment? In this critical instant of an "ontological event" that remains an abiding trauma to the modern imagination, the Doctor mutters something about his never having time now to remove his friend's diseased gall bladder. Do we have a right to expect more, before we bestow the laurel of insight upon *Holocaust*?

Could Gerald Green and his producers have done better? Consider this brief portrait of two human beings, about to die in the gas chambers

of Auschwitz, recorded by Salmen Lewental in a diary exhumed from the
ashes after the war:

> A mother was sitting with her daughter, they both spoke in
> Polish. She sat helplessly, spoke so softly that she could hardly be
> heard. She was clasping the head of her daughter with her hands
> and hugging her tightly. [She spoke]: "In an hour we shall die.
> What a tragedy. My dearest, my last hope will die with you." She
> sat . . . immersed in thought, with wide-open, dimmed eyes . . .
> After some minutes she came to and continued to speak. "On
> account of you my pain is so great that I am dying when I think
> of it." She let down her stiff arms and her daughter's head sank
> down upon her mother's knees. A shiver passed through the body
> of the young girl, she called desperately "Mama!" And she spoke
> no more, those were her last words.

Perhaps "last words" like these are not dramatic; certainly they are not
commercial; undoubtedly, they are not American. But they are authentic, and
they are what the Holocaust was all about. The upbeat ending of *Holocaust*,
minimizing the negative impact of all that has gone before, typifies the
absence of insight and the externalization of horror that makes the entire
production meretricious in its confrontation with disaster: wormwood and
gall are mollified by aromatic spices from the orient. To leave an audience of
millions with an image like the one of mother and daughter bereft of hope,
of life, of speech would have been too dark—too dark altogether. The American theater and screen, the American mind itself, is not yet ready to end in
such silence. The heroic gesture still seizes us with its glamour, tempering
the doom of men and women who have lost control of their fate. Salmen
Lewental has recorded an epigraph for all writing about victims of the Holocaust, whether as art or history—and it may serve as epitaph too: "On
account of you my pain is so great that I am dying when I think of it." The
memory of eleven million dead echoes as a symphony of pain: in that denial
of final triumph lies our acceptance and understanding of the Holocaust
experience.

YASMINE ERGAS

Growing up Banished: A Reading of Anne Frank and Etty Hillesum

Memories help us live. Oddly, they need not be our own, seared as they are into the lives of those who were not there. Wars, for example: long after the bombing has stopped and the shell-shocked cities have been reconstructed, children learn to remember scenes of devastation they never witnessed. Persecution, too: age-old fears come to haunt generations born and bred in safety. Partly experienced and partly borrowed, memories are selective—mental notebooks we keep to honor the past, but equally to keep track of ourselves. "*Remember what it was to be me*: that is always the point," Joan Didion said of her jottings, and the same could well be said of what we choose to recall.

Diaries serve a double function, reminding both author and reader of a past self. Anne Frank and Etty Hillesum tracked their personal routes along transitory moments, and we in turn trace in their diaries the signposts to the present. Although the differences between then and now, between them and us, are enormous, these diaries still feed the memories of many today.

An Interrupted Life and *The Diary of a Young Girl* bear witness to life as it was lived in parallel to the Nazi concentration camps. They are not "camp" stories, permeated by the horrors of Auschwitz or Dachau. Instead, they tell of the attempt to maintain or construct normalcy in a rapidly bestializing civil society. From them we learn of persecution and war as they once intertwined with the processes of growing up female and Jewish.

From *Behind the Lines: Gender and the Two World Wars* by Yasmine Ergas. © 1987 by Yale University Press. Reprinted by permission of Yale University Press.

What do they tell us? Synopses of such works are always difficult. For portrayals of the authors, let me refer you to the texts themselves. My intent is to unravel something of what they say about developing identities in the context of genocide. The diaries talk of maintaining individuality, forging personalities, coming to terms with femininity when persecution straitjackets its victims into a racial identity intended to be all-encompassing and all-defining. Although Anne Frank and Etty Hillesum repeatedly attempt to fashion and review their ways of being women, gender ultimately recedes to second place. As Nazism casts them, they must cast themselves: first and foremost as Jews.

These diaries speak, then, of the intersection of war and persecution. War is not for everyone the same. For persecuted groups, its contours are dictated by banishment. Their men and boys do not defend their countries at the front; they are not the nation's warriors. Their women and girls do not courageously nurse the wounded in battle, send their beloveds patriotic messages sealed with state approval, or otherwise join the country's effort. They may escape, resist, or submit. But they must always confront the condition of having been singled out—in this case, for annihilation.

Both young women, relatively affluent, of cultured milieux, and trapped in German-occupied Holland, Etty and Anne recorded the passages that led from individual lives to a collective fate. Etty Hillesum began writing first, at the age of twenty-seven. Her diaries, abridged by her Dutch publisher, were written between March, 1941, and October, 1942. The book also includes a few letters written later, up until her deportation on September 7, 1943. When Anne Frank started her diary on June 14, 1942, Etty was close to ending her own. And by the time the Frank household was deported—on August 4, 1944—Etty has been dead in Auschwitz, eight months.

Their styles are very different. Anne receives a diary for her thirteenth birthday. Within a week the diary has acquired a name, Kitty, and been properly introduced, via Anne's descriptions, to the entire family. Kitty is Anne's confidante in a friendship initiated in freedom and continued in the cloistered captivity of the *Achterhuis* or Secret Annexe where the family, together with a colleague of Otto Frank's, Mr. Van Daan, his wife, and their adolescent son, Peter, find refuge. (Some time after going into hiding, they invited Albert Dussel, a dentist of late middle age, to join them.) Notwithstanding occasional doubts, Anne possesses the "instinct for reality" that is the hallmark of a diary keeper. Everyday life is not too prosaic to be carefully recorded. She chronicles its details, patterning the day's events into a coherent narrative. The narrative is its own point, although it also often serves as the springboard for moral reflections, laying the foundations of *Selbstbildung*, of construction of the self or of self-improvement.

Etty hardly ever reports a day's events and never provides an introduction to her cast of characters. Like a diver going off the deep end, she
plunges in with "Here goes, then." A series of reflections follows, written
at all times of day and night. Etty is not addressing a paper stand-in for a
best friend as she records impressions and feelings in a nervous reworking
of her spiritual and moral self. Her diaries are written in the mode of anno-
tations designed to evoke a full range of associations rather than to record
each day's passing. "That may seem rather clumsily put, but I know what I
mean," she comments after a particularly elliptical entry, making the point
of her writing clear.

A variety of factors must have contributed to the two women's diver-
gent approaches. The one conjures up her alter ego as an imaginary penpal,
while the other seeks to fathom and reorder her innermost self. For Etty,
turning inward is painful: "So many inhibitions," she remarks at the outset,
"so much fear of letting go, of allowing things to pour out of me, and yet that
is what I must do if I am ever to give my life a reasonable and satisfactory
purpose. It is like the final, liberating scream that always sticks bashfully in
your throat when you make love." For Anne, the diary is an immediate
source of joy: "Now I must stop. Bye-bye, we're going to great pals!" she
ends her first entry.

Despite their differences, Anne and Etty share a propensity to harp on
the limitations inherent in women's attitudes toward men and to set themselves on routes of less fettered freedom. For Anne, the captive community
in which she lives provides the models from whom she fully intends to differ:
her mother, Mrs. Van Daan, even her much-admired sister. The pettiness of
their concerns strikes her, as does the triviality of their accomplishments. "If
God lets me live," she exclaims in April, 1944, "I shall attain more than
Mummy has ever done, I shall not remain insignificant." A few days earlier
she remarked in a similar vein: "I want to get on; I can't imagine that I would
have to lead the same sort of life as Mummy and Mrs. Van Daan and all the
women who do their work and are forgotten." The road to significance leads,
Anne thinks, through working "in the world and for mankind"; the road to
life after death, she hopes, can be paved by writing. Femininity rarely
threatens these aspirations: there are no obvious traces of female fear of
success. Just before scorning her mother's "insignificance," Ann affirms
confidence in herself. "I know what I want, I have a goal, an opinion, I have
a religion and love. Let me be myself and then I am satisfied. I know that I'm
a woman, a woman with inward strength and plenty of courage."

Like Anne, Etty is impatient with the conventional bonds of womanhood. While also referring critically to her mother, she frequently proffers
general comments on the "not at all simple . . . role of women," whose marks

she recognizes in herself—unlike Anne. Passing "a beautiful, well-groomed, wholly feminine, albeit dull woman, I completely lose my poise. Then I feel that my intellect, my struggle, my suffering, are oppressive, ugly, unwomanly; then I, too, want to be beautiful and dull, a desirable plaything for a man." This desiring to be desired Etty dismisses as "only a primitive instinct." Reflecting on traditional feminine conditioning, she looks forward to an "essential emancipation of women." "We still have to be born as human beings, that is the great task that lies before us."

This want of emancipation notwithstanding, Etty's lifestyle seems largely unhampered by patriarchal constraints. Her reviewers often cite as indictors of her sexual liberty her dual involvement with her mentor, Speier, and Papa Han, her kindly and elderly landlord; and her entries allude to several earlier experiences. She pursued her psychological and spiritual liberation in tandem with her studies. Having already earned a degree in law at the University of Amsterdam, she enrolled in the Faculty of Slavonic Languages before turning to psychology. She lived in Papa Han's house with four friends, in an arrangement similar to that often found around university campuses today. The way to free femininity may have been arduous and uncharted, but it was open. So it appeared, at least, as described by Anne and Etty, upper-middle-class girls of "enlightened" and cultured backgrounds. But, while the future of women revealed avenues of possibility, that of the Jews appeared increasingly walled in by political foreclosures.

Branded as a special enemy in occupied lands, the Jews were sharply set off from their societies. As the racial laws were strengthened, demarcations became more rigid. Race prevailed as the ordering societal criterion. Yet Etty had been keeping a diary for six months before she talked of herself as a Jew, and even then the mention is more metaphorical than factual. On walking through south Amsterdam, she wrote, "I felt like an old Jew, wrapped up in a cloud. No doubt that's recorded somewhere in our mythology: a Jew moving along, wrapped up in a cloud." Over the course of many months, however, her Jewishness impinges on her sense of self at an accelerating pace, finally becoming the implicit referent when she says *we*. For Etty, "Jew"— once a seemingly marginal connotation—had been transformed into the incalculable answer to the question "who am I?" In July, 1942, she wrote: "What is at stake is our impending destruction and annihilation, we can have no more illusions about that. They are out to destroy us completely, we must accept that and go on from there."

A fortnight earlier, Anne had introduced herself to the as yet unnamed Kitty. "Sketching in the brief story of my life," a sentence and a half sufficed for the family's vital statistics: her parents' ages at marriage, the births of her elder sister, Margot, and of herself. Immediately she launched into a description of their lives, "as we are Jewish." Friday evening dinners or Passover festivities do not ensue. Of the forty-five lines that Anne dedicates to this presentation, thirty are devoted to the Nazi racial laws and their repercussions. "As we are Jewish," Anne explains, the Franks had left Germany in 1933. But the rest of the family had stayed behind, "so life was filled with anxiety." With the arrival of the Germans in Holland, "the suffering of us Jews really began. Anti-Jewish decrees followed each other in quick succession," and she lists them. To be a Jew, a persecuted Jew, is an essential component of Anne's sense of self: it prescribes the coordinates by which she locates herself in the world.

Anne chafes against the racial yoke represented by the yellow star. "Surely the time will come when we are people again, and not just Jews," she writes well into 1944, longing not for the obliteration of Jewish identity but for the restoration of individuality. Etty invokes that time too, in a letter from Westerbrok. "The outside world probably thinks of us as a grey, uniform, suffering mass of Jews, and knows nothing of the gulfs and abysses and subtle differences that exist between us. They could never hope to understand." To understand, that is, how differences persist notwithstanding the iron rule of racial caste.

Collective identities imply common destinies. As the Nazi persecution intensified, the futures Anne and Etty envisaged changed. In April, 1942, Etty could anticipate the day when, chancing upon an anemone preserved in the pages of her diary, she would remember Speier's fifty-fifth birthday. Looking back upon this happy moment of her youth, she would then be, Etty foresaw, a matron who had attained a clearly imagined moment of the future. That future represented a personal development woven from the idiosyncratic yearnings of an aspiring writer endowed with intense spiritualist tendencies and strong passions. "I am sure," she wrote in the early summer, "that one day I shall go to the East." But within a matter of weeks the prospect of walking through Japanese landscapes had faded. The future was reduced to the question of survival or death as persecution crystallized the awareness that reordered experience, the anticipation of imminent mass murder. On "July 3, 1942, Friday evening, 8:30" she describes the rupture that has sundered her life's apparent continuities. "Yes, I am still at the same desk, but it seems to me that I am going to have to draw a line under everything and continue in a different tone." "Every day I shall put my papers in order and every day I shall say farewell."

Anne undergoes a similar transition. In the summer of 1944 the young girl who "did so want to grow into a real young woman" senses her impending doom and recalls her obligations. "I must uphold my ideals, for perhaps the time will come when I shall be able to carry them out," she reminds herself, having stared disaster in the face. "I see the world gradually being turned into a wilderness. I hear the ever approaching thunder, which will destroy us too, I can feel the suffering of millions and yet, if I look up into the heavens, I think that it will all come right." Months earlier, she had equated the time when it would "all come right" with survival and testimony. In April she had written: "If we bear all this suffering and if there are still Jews left, when it is over, then Jews instead of being doomed will be held up as an example." Distinguishing herself from Margot, who wished to be a midwife in Palestine, Anne dreamed that May of a year in Paris and one in London, learning languages and studying the history of art, seeing "beautiful dresses" and "doing all kinds of exciting things." Hopes of an individual, lighthearted future remained, hostage of an uncertain collective fate.

The leaden quality of that fate contrasted sharply with the possibilities feminine identity seemed to hold in store. Reading Anne and Etty it seems, however, that persecution provided a greater impetus to searches that stretched Jewish spirituality than to social experiments that yielded transformative models of femininity. Bound to a hunted community at once racial and religious, Anne and Etty seek the transcendental meaning that can endow their lives with reason, value, and significance. In a novel written in hiding, Anne grapples with the divisiveness of race. The tale of Cady—who appears in many ways indistinguishable from her narrator—breaks off in grief when the heroine's friend Mary is deported. "'Mary, forgive me, come back.' Cady no longer knew what to say or think. For this misery she saw so clearly before her eyes there were no words . . . she saw a troop of armed brutes . . . and in among them, helpless and alone, Mary, Mary who was the same as she was."

Anne's fiction echoes her diary. On November 26, 1943, she dreamed of her deported school friend, Lies. Lies's imploring gaze mesmerized Anne, now anguished and incapable of offering help, wracked by grief and an emotion we term today "survivor's guilt." Like Anne in her dream, Cady ranks among the privileged. But between them there is an important distinction: Cady is a Christian. As Anne's double on the other side of the racial divide, she incarnates a pedagogy of the persecuted. A Christian emphasizing anti-Semitism's savagery, she epitomizes the moral stance Anne must have recognized in the Christian friends on whose unfaltering loyalty the Secret Annexe depended. Anne became conscious of the growing precariousness of such a stance when the news of spreading, virulent Dutch anti-Semitism reached the family's refuge. Insisting that "one must always look at things from both sides," she tried to explain to Kitty the alleged behavior of those Jews who, by betraying resistance secrets or otherwise acting wrongly, had incurred the wrath of the Germans on the Netherlands. Anne did look at things from both sides, through Cady: as a Jew taking on the persona of a Christian and as a Christian seeing herself in the person of a Jew.

Strikingly, in this only fictional piece to mention Jews, Anne does not clearly identify as one herself. Here the *Tales* and the *Diary* differ: with the exception of Cady's story, Anne refrains from literary forays into the matter of her own race. But, although no one ever utters a *kiddush*, religiosity surfaces throughout fables and short stories animated by Anne's psychological twins: fairies, elves, bears, and little girls. Belief in God repeatedly issues from their voyages in search of self. "In the field, amid the flowers, beneath the darkening sky, Krista is content. Gone is fatigue . . . the little girl dreams and thinks only of the bliss of having, each day, this short while alone with God and nature." The first-person protagonist of "Fear" comes to a similar conclusion. Having fled her city home in the midst of violent bombings, she finally rests in the countryside. Later, when war is over, fear appears as "a sickness for which there is only one remedy . . . look at nature and see that God is much closer than most people think." Locked into the Secret Annexe, Anne could not indulge longings for nature and personal space. The claustrophobic world of confinement forced the quest for meaning—and identity—inward.

Exploring spirituality introspectively and untrammeled by religious observance, Anne developed beliefs at most loosely related to Judaism. Embracing practices and systems of signification proper to Christianity, Etty even more evidently strained the limits of received religion. The morning of Good Friday, 1942, she recounts having knelt in prayer and recalls the bathroom's "rough coconut matting." Hesitantly, she confesses to success, for the struggle to bow down in prayer has long engaged her and is central to the allegory she has been weaving, the tale of "the girl who could not kneel." In October of that year she equates kneeling with prayer. Her story, she says is strange: "the girl who could not kneel. Or its variation: the girl who could not pray." Like her practices, her beliefs assume Christian tonalities. "I have broken my body like bread and shared it out among men. And why not, they were hungry and had gone without for so long," the last diary entry notes before her sacrificial closing words: "We should be willing to act as balm for all wounds." The Christian hues of her faith notwithstanding, Etty never disavows Judaism, nor does she dwell on its potential conflicts with her spiritual trajectory. On the contrary, referring to her love for Speier she exclaimed at the end of April, 1942, "I am so glad that he is a Jew and I a Jewess."

While the grip of racial Jewishness tightened, its hold as an organized religion weakened. Practice was largely impossible. The Franks, who took a menorah into hiding, complemented Chanukah candle-lightings with

Christmas celebrations. Perhaps privileged Dutch and German Jews like Etty or Anne were already too distant from the Jewish religious tradition to perpetuate it in such trying conditions and on their own. And yet, Anne's father oversaw her nightly prayers. Many factors must have fashioned their spiritualities. Certainly, persecuted Jews found innumerable solutions to the question all were asking: "God Almighty, what are You doing to us?" The words escaped Etty in Westerbrok.

Somehow, every Jew had to find an answer. And every answer found remained that of a Jew. No matter how apostate individual Jews' beliefs, the Nazi persecution had established the supremacy of descent over faith in the definition of the Jewish community. For all her spiritual trespassing into Christian domains, Etty, like Anne, stayed within that community. In the practical activity of evolving beliefs, with untold others they explored possible religiosities of the unobservant Jew.

By contrast, persecution provided Anne and Etty with few opportunities for the practical remodeling of their identities as women. Where soldiers are drawn from populations neatly cleaved along lines of gender, age, and health, when war leads able-bodied men to battle and leaves all others at home, persecuted groups are promiscuously amassed into communities of fear. Nazi anti-Semitism did not emancipate Jewish women. Slave labor cannot be equated with enlistment for factory jobs or other patriotic—and remunerative—tasks. For Jewish women, barriers affecting labor-force participation were not lifted. They were not called upon to occupy posts men left vacant. They were not integrated into labor organizations. They did not axiomatically gain special powers over their households, head communities and families, bring in vital wages, reorganize living arrangements, support dependents. They were not awarded childcare services, nutrition programs, widows' pensions. They were not extolled by ideologies that elevated their status while catalyzing their support. In their struggles to survive extermina-tion, Jewish women often found themselves alone, responsible for the shelter of others, or otherwise pivotal to collective moral and material economies. Nazism undid the patriarchal family as it ripped apart the fabric of Jewish life. But gender roles were not systematically rewoven by women darning the holes that men's absences opened. War befits women, some have argued, pitching bellicose Minervas and triumphant Nikes against romantic portrayals of pacifist Geas. At a minimum, they claim, war has benefited women in the twentieth century and the West. Yet neither economically nor socially nor politically did the Nazi war reallocate power to Jewish women.

Persecution brought Etty a new job as a clerical employee of the Jewish Council, with its attendant emotional responsibilities toward the deportees with whom she worked and lived at Westerbrok. Lowly as her position may have been in the Council's hierarchy, it conferred petty powers and offered her temporary security. But it also tainted her with the guilt of collaboration and of that, too, she was sporadically aware. Before entering into this Nazi-created employment, Etty had worked, earned money, and overseen her own living arrangements. As a woman, under Nazism, she never gained; as a Jew, she only lost.

Anne lost too. Like others in hiding or attempting escape, the Franks lived within a drastically narrowed circle of social relations. Here familial or quasi-familial bonds strengthened into clandestine enclaves of solidarity. With everyone's safety at the mercy of the others' fealty and sense of responsibility, a general flattening of social status ensued. The Secret Annexe housed an extended ménage that partially reshuffled gender roles. Otto Frank and Mr. Van Daan peeled potatoes alongside their wives: testimony more to the loss of their external, head-of-the-household functions than to their wives' elevation. However, many other tasks retained their conventional gender markings. Protection, for example, remained a manly duty. Peeling potatoes and protecting the household need not clash, and in the Annexe clandestine life restricted role-playing and the potential for role conflict.

In this context of limited activity, there were few occasions for Anne to realize her emancipatory desires. Her diary and short stories provided writing practice, an informal apprenticeship for the career she wished to undertake. Lessons, from math to shorthand, broadened the scope of her abilities. Her mother proved a source of frustration and rivalry, her father of affection, Mrs. Van Daan of contempt, and Albert Dussel of irritation. With Peter, the Van Daans' adolescent son, she navigated through a sentimental journey clouded by parental disapproval. Yet all these elements spurring Anne's development pale by comparison to her world before confinement or even to the war-ridden world of her non-Jewish peers. Stripped of every right, amid the debris of their decimated milieux, Anne and Etty were killed. Women, but most of all Jews, on every possible count for them Nazism and war entailed losing.

As the persecuted resist the progressive diminishment of self, they struggle against the temporal scansions that are imposed upon them. They do not walk in step with the drumbeat of battle and bombs. For persecution proceeds at its own pace, and the persecuted are mobilized not to the call of the nation but to the cumulation of special prohibitions and obligations. Some, like Anne and her family, meticulously plan for invasion. For over a year, the Franks stocked food, clothes, and furniture in the Secret Annexe. Or, like Etty, they tenaciously cling to everyday life. "I cannot take in how beautiful the jasmine is," she wrote on July 1, 1942, "but there is no need to.

It is enough simply to believe in miracles in the 20th century. And I do, even though the lice will be eating me up in Poland before long." Others join the Resistance, engaging their oppressors in armed struggle. No matter which stance they take, persecution, more than war, orders their public experience.

Persecution imposes its measure on personal time, too. Anne divided life into before, during, and after hiding. Memory reigned over "before." Routines provided a modicum of activity to make time pass in the present. Her passion for Peter, like the radio broadcasts announcing the war's events, anticipated a time to come "after." Ultimately, writing for both Etty and Anne bridged the time of persecution and that which followed, transforming their diaries from tools of authorial apprenticeship into testimonials to the present and instruments of its transcendence. Etty kept her diary to remain her "own witness, marking well everything that happens in this world." She was determined to "know this century of ours inside and out" and describe it. Finally, her diary condensed her aspirations, the legacy she bequeathed in fulfillment of a promise made in the summer of 1942, when she vowed: "When I have survived it all, I shall write stories about these times that will be like faint brush strokes against the great wordless background of God, Life, Death, Suffering, and Eternity." Anne, too, planned a testimonial, hoping "to publish a book entitled *Het Achterhuis* after the war"—the book her diary became.

Tales of persecution are crucial to the European memory of World War II. It is a memory periodically fanned by the celebrations of antifascist resistances (where they existed), national holidays, the capture or escape of a Nazi war criminal. And by a few, enduring testimonies. Such testimonies are provided by the *Diary of Anne Frank* and Etty Hillesum's *An Interrupted Life*. Like many memoirs of war, they bespeak a remote "other" path to, or through, adulthood: one produced by fragments of past normalities as they shatter into conflict and loss. But, unlike war literature at large, these memoirs evoke the specific horror of anti-Semetic persecution four decades ago. Their protagonists have become emblematic of the journey through banishment and exile that so frequently ended in death. Their words resonate today, and not simple because they left lessons about our possible tomorrows. Rather, they resonate because we remember, and what we remember colors who we are.

SANDER L. GILMAN

The Dead Child Speaks:
Reading The Diary of Anne Frank

N*o single document* written during the Holocaust riveted the attention of
the Western reading public more than the diary kept by Anne Frank and
published in extract by her father, Otto in 1947. Translated from the original
Dutch into French in 1950, these extracts were initially read by a relatively
small audience. Even the 1950 German translation had no resonance. It was
only with its publication in the United States in 1952 that the diary was
brought to the attention of a wider reading public. The English stage adaptation in 1955 inspired a republication of the German translation by the
house of S. Fischer, and this caught the imagination of the German reading
public. The German critic Philip Wiebe, writing in the socialist *World of
Work* in 1955, summarized the German response to the discovery that the
Jews murdered in the Holocaust were not passive and silent about their fate:
"When we read the publisher's note about her dreadful death, we feel a true
pain about the tragic fate of this young Jewess, who, through her jottings, has
become better known to us than our sister." The Western reading public, in
Germany as well as in the United States, came to measure the Holocaust
through its identification with the individual fate of Anne Frank. Untangling
the reading of this text presents some extraordinary complications, complications resulting from the fragmentary nature of *The Diary's* publication as
well as from its reception in the light of its dramatization. Anne Frank

From *Studies in American Jewish Literature* 7:1 (Spring 1988). © 1988 by The Kent State
University Press. Reprinted with permission of The Kent State University Press.

provided a ready-made definition of the Jew as author, and the Jewish author as mute victim after the Holocaust.

The complexity of reading *The Diary of Anne Frank* can be measured by its function in any number of studies of the Holocaust written by German Jewish survivors during the late 1950s. Theodor Adorno, in an essay on the reconstruction of the past, used an anecdote concerning the dramatization of *The Diary* to show the limitations of texts in uncovering the true nature of the Holocaust and its origin. He reports that he had been told of a woman in Germany who had seen the production of the stage version of *The Diary* and had said afterwards, deeply moved: "Yes, but *that* girl at least should have been allowed to live." Adorno sees this as a tentative first step to an awareness of the nature of the Holocaust, but an awareness that, "although it seems to trivialize the dead," is limited by its focus on a single case and avoids any search for the cause of the tragedy. What Adorno does not read into this response is the inherent ambivalence of the statement, for it is possible to read it as stating: "We were in general right to kill them, but in this specific case we should have behaved differently." Adorno, himself a survivor who escaped Germany in 1934, sees here as faulty the focus on the individual as the means of escaping any search for the true roots of the Holocaust. He also shows how the Germans remain unmoved even by this individual fate to examine their own basic attitudes toward the Jews. George Steiner, in his essay on the "hollow miracle," echoes this view: "True, German audiences were moved not long ago by the dramatization of *The Diary of Anne Frank*. But even the terror of *The Diary* has been an exceptional reminder. And it does not show what happened to Anne *inside* the camp. There is little market for such things in Germany." The drama based on *The Diary* provided the audience in Germany as well as throughout the Western world with a living victim. It provided the resurrection of one of the dead witnesses of the Holocaust, one who spoke and thus broke through the silence attributed to the victim.

The relationship between *The Diary* and the play is important for understanding the movement of the text from the world of the text to that of "realistic illusion," the world of the theater. It also provides the frame for one of the most striking images of the "self-hating" Jew to be found in post-Holocaust writing. In 1950 the Jewish American writer Meyer Levin read the French translation of the diary. Levin, a lifelong Zionist, had authored, in 1931, the first English novel dealing with the kibbutz movement. Convinced that *The Diary* was the living witness to the Holocaust, "the voice from the mass grave," he reviewed it in the *Congress Weekly*, the organ of the American Jewish Congress, and his review led to the publication of the English translation by Doubleday. Levin thus received permission from Anne Frank's father, Otto, to write the stage adaptation. When the dramatization was finished, it was passed on to the producer, Cheryl Crawford, who rejected it, at least in part on the advice of the dramatist Lillian Hellman, as unplayable. The project eventually passed into the hands of Kermit Bloomgarden, who, again with the advice of Hellman, commissioned the husband-and-wife team of Frances Goodrich and Albert Hackett to write a new adaptation of *The Diary*, which was performed in 1955 and won the Pulitzer prize. Starring Susan Strasberg, it was the hit of the 1955–56 Broadway season. In 1959 Millie Perkins was cast as Anne Frank in George Stevens's film version of the play, with Joseph Schildkraut as Otto Frank. The success of the film imprinted the figure of Anne Frank as the image of the victim on international awareness. The motion picture, with all of its sense of the need for a commercial success among groups other than Jews, maintained the sanitized version of Goodrich and Hackett and added to it many of the banalities of Hollywood's post-Holocaust image of the Jew as victim. Anne Frank becomes a positive figure through being the essential victim in a manner parallel to that of the figure of Noah Ackerman (played by Montgomery Clift) in Edward Dmytryk's 1958 film of Irwin Shaw's *The Young Lions* or Danny Kaye's comic S.L. Jacobowsky in the film version of Franz Werfel's *Me and the Colonel* (1958). Jews are victims—positive victims, but victims nevertheless. This short history of the creation of the dramatization is of importance only in that it sets the stage for one of the most complex creations of a projection of self-hatred by a twentieth-century Jewish writer. From 1953 to 1957 Meyer Levin instituted a series of lawsuits against the producer of the play as well as Otto Frank. In January 1958 Levin was awarded fifty thousand dollars in damages.

Levin's struggle with *The Diary*, a text that had a central position in his understanding of the Holocaust in the history of Western Jewry, and his projection of the "bad" Jew formed the basis for a novel, *The Fanatic* (1964), and the second volume of his autobiography, *The Obsession* (1973). The first volume of his autobiography, *In Search* (1950), ended with the founding of the state of Israel; the second volume, initially entitled "The Manipulators," dealt exclusively with *The Diary* and his role in presenting it to the world. This autobiographical text is remarkable, for, like Elias Canetti's memoirs, it is as much an attempt to provide a reading of a series of actions as it is an attempt to present them. The "frame" of the autobiography is Levin's psychoanalysis, which is aimed at his trying to understand the basis for his "obsession" with the diary. Levin sees his exclusion from participation in the presentation of *The Diary* to the living world of the theater as the result of a plot on the part of the German Jewish Communist intelligentsia. He focuses on Lillian Hellman, born in New Orleans of German Jewish ancestry, blacklisted under McCarthy, and one of the most visible representatives of American liberalism on the Broadway stage, as the essential "bad" Jew. He sees her as manipulating *The Diary* to stress its "international" rather than its specifically Jewish character. His dramatization of the diary was unacceptable, he believes, because it was "too Jewish." The "bad" Jew, that Jew which Levin wishes to distance from himself, is the German Jew, the international Jew:

> It was true . . . that although Otto [Frank] was entirely unpre-
> tentious, something of the aristocratic manner remained, despite
> even the experience of Auschwitz—and, nasty as this seems—I
> must put down that even on that day there arose in me a faint
> doubt as to his view of me, a doubt that I once suppressed with
> shame, as being due to my early Chicago prejudices against
> German Jews, who persisted in their superiority-attitude toward
> us *Ostjuden* from Poland or Russia. . . .To this day I accuse myself
> of this counter-prejudice against German Jews, yet I cannot rid
> myself of the feeling that I am seen by them as a Yid.

Levin uncovers the fact that the Franks were indeed a wealthy, highly assim-ilated family in Frankfurt before they emigrated to the Netherlands. Indeed, he further discovered that they were related to the Straus family (which owned Macy's) and that Otto Frank had spent a year in New York working for them. The German Jewish conspiracy is thus complete.

Levin's need is to mold Anne Frank and her text into a "Jewish"—that is, anti-assimilationist—model, for he sees in the assimilation of the German Jews, of Frank herself, a fault that can only be rectified by a return to his own sense of what is appropriate for *the* witness to the torment of the Jews. Frank must be made to speak as a Jew, and Jews, having been treated as different, must see themselves as positively different. The "Hellman-Hackett" version of *The Diary* (as Levin refers to it throughout the text) stressed the univer-salism of Anne Frank. Thus their text altered a passage that stressed the difference of the Jews ("Who has made us Jews different from all other people . . . If we bear all this suffering and if there are still Jews left, when it is over, then Jews, instead of being doomed, will be held up as an example.") into one that stated their representative function as victims ("We're not the only people that've had to suffer. There have always been people that've had to . . . sometimes one race . . . sometimes another."). For Levin this alter-ation, which made Anne Frank the representative of yet another example of humankind's inhumanity to humans rather than of specifically German persecution of the Jews, smacks of the assimilationsist tendency that views him as merely a "Yid." The world of the German Jew is corrupt and degenerate.

While one may wish to see Levin's attack on the universalization of Anne Frank's experience as a means of protecting the "Jewish" character of the Holocaust, it is clear that the Franks' brand of ethnic Judaism was inherently unacceptable to Levin. "Jewish," is for him, a narrowly defined label which would preclude precisely the type of universalization advocated by German Jews such as the Franks and which echoes very clearly in the dramatization. Levin reproduces this image of the corrupt German Jew in great detail in his best-known work, his novelization of the Leopold-Loeb murder case, in which he presents the world of Chicago's German Jewish community as one that produces unmotivated murders not unlike those of Nazi Germany. *Compulsion* (1956) was a work that he hoped would "show what those overproud German Jews, with their superiority and their exclusiveness, were like."

Both the Hackett dramatization of *The Diary of Anne Frank* and Levin's seemed to present antithetical readings of a text in the light of two models of the Jew present in Eisenhower's America. The first was of the Jew as a child, as victim, like all other children, like all other victims. The only answer to this image was the liberal answer: Humanity must eliminate all suffering, and such suffering, too, would vanish. How? The underlying theme of the drama is certainly not a Marxist one. There is no intimation that anti-Semitism (or indeed any other persecution) is the result of a decaying world of capitalism. Rather the audience is left with the vague feeling that something must be done, even if no program is presented. Levin's reading presents a program. It is through the strong identification of Jews as political and religious Jews, defined in the light of the newly realized political ideal of Zionism, that such horrors can be prevented from happening again. *The Diary* itself, or at least the fragments that have been published, presents a mix of both views. But Levin's selective reading of these fragments reveals strikingly his wish to label Anne Frank as the "good" Jew, and thus the "good" Jew as writer, and his parallel wish to see in Hellman the "bad" Jew as writer. One of the central proofs that Levin brought in his court suit against the Hacketts was the use of a specific scene placed at the conclusion of the second act: "Here, now, was the Chanukah scene, just as I had placed it, as the climax at the close of the second act. Anne, extremely excited, hurrying about distributing her little gifts, the excitement mounting and mounting—something seemed wrong to me. The way they had done it was more like Christmas." Indeed, the Chanukah celebration is so presented in the Hacketts' play. But what is the parallel in the diary itself? On 7 December, 1942, Anne Frank record that Chanukah and St. Nicholas's Day fell almost together. Chanukah was celebrated, but "the evening of St. Nicholas's Day was much more fun." In December 1943 there are five separate entries recording her joy at the coming of St. Nicolas's Day and Christmas. It is on St. Nicholas's Day that good little boys and girls are rewarded with gifts, while bad children receive coals in their shoes. Anne Frank was typical of assimilated Jews, who adopted Christian religious observations without any religious overtones in lieu of a Jewish religious celebration. Both versions of the play thus create a speaking Jew, and being Jewish, at least in the world of the theater, is tied to the image of religion, if not to religion itself. The language that Anne Frank is made to speak is stage English, just as her diary was written in literary Dutch, so there is not specific linguistic marker for her identity. She does not speak with a Jewish accent, does not mix bits of Hebrew in her discourse. The authors, no matter what their political persuasion, must give her some type of identification as a Jew. For the illusion is that the Jewish dead of the Holocaust are made to speak. This is, of course, merely an illusion. The dead remain mute; the living revivify them for their own ends.

Early in his recounting of his involvement with the dramatization of *The Diary*, Meyer Levin cites one authority whose work on the pattern of survival has become a standard in the past decades. Bruno Bettelheim, born and educated in Vienna, was incarcerated in Dachau and Buchenwald during 1938 and 1939. His study *The Informed Heart* (1960) was his attempt to see the Holocaust as an outgrowth of modern society. He views the inability of the Jews to respond to the world of the camps as merely another manifestation of the dehumanization of modern technological society. As early as 1943 Bettelheim expressed this view in one of the first psychological studies of the Nazi persecution of the Jews. But it was only in 1960, after the tremendous success of the dramatization of *The Diary of Anne Frank*, that Bettelheim produced a monograph on the Holocaust, a monograph that contained a study of *The Diary*. In it Bettelheim criticizes Otto Frank for putting his family into hiding and maintaining, in their hiding place, the idea that life must continue "as nearly as possible in the usual fashion." Bettelheim castigates the Franks for not hiding individually or providing themselves with weapons to resist their (for Bettelheim) inevitable discovery and deportation. Bettelheim's criticism of the reception of *The Diary* is aimed at those who wish "to forget the gas chambers and to glorify attitudes of extreme privatization, of continuing to hold onto attitudes as usual even in a Holocaust." He sees the popularity of the book as a part of the denial "that Auschwitz even exisited. If all men are good there was never an Auschwitz." This is the final line of the Hacketts' dramatization. Meyer Levin cites Bettelheim as his authority on survival, since he survived the camp experience. He sees him as the "good" survivor whose work exposes the "bad" survivor, Otto Frank, whose actions caused the death of the "good" Jew, Anne Frank. Similarly, George Steiner sees in Bettelheim's study the inner truth of the Holocaust because of his claim to authentic personal experience: "Fiction falls silent before the enormity of the fact, and before the vivid authority with which that fact can be rendered by unadorned report."

Indeed, Bettelheim himself, in his 1979 collection of essays pointedly called *Surviving*, republished his 1960 essay "The Ignored Lesson of Anne Frank." It becomes clear that Bettelheim too is responding to the "speaking" Anne Frank of the drama, at the conclusion of which she says, in a disembodied voice, "In spite of everything, I still believe that people are really good at heart." "This improbable sentiment is supposedly from a girl who had been starved to death, had watched her sister meet the same fate before she did, knew that her mother had been murdered, and had watched untold thousands of adults and children actually being killed. The statement is not justified by anything Anne actually told her diary." Bettelheim implies that he knows that the opposite must have been true—that Anne Frank must have lost her individuality in the camps, that she, too, must have been dehumanized. Of course this is as much a subjective reading as that of the Hacketts. Bettelheim's pessimistic reading of Anne Frank's fate is needed by him to explain her failure to survive. Indeed, in the 1960 essay, Bettelheim compares Anne Frank's diary with the autobiography of another survivor, Marga Minco, whose *Bitter Herbs* appeared in 1960. Bettelheim is appalled at the "universal admiration of [the Franks'] way of coping, or rather of not coping. The story of little Marga who survived, every bit as touching, remains totally neglected by comparison." It is the living survivor, Bettelheim himself, who is neglected, while the voices of the dead continue to haunt him. Bettelheim's reworking of the earlier excursus on Anne Frank in this later essay repeats many of the earlier claims. It lays directly on the doorstep of the "play and movie" the denial of the realities of the Holocaust: "If all men are good at heart, there never really was an Auschwitz; nor is there any possibility that it may recur." Bettelheim has created in his image of Anne Frank the source of the denial of the Holocaust, of the father as the "bad" Jew, of the speaking witness as the lying witness.

In January 1959, while Bettelheim was writing his long essay on Anne Frank, a German schoolteacher named Lothar Stielau was charged with disseminating anti-Semitic propaganda. Stielau, a member of a neo-Nazi party in Lübeck, had claimed that *The Diary of Anne Frank* was a fabrication, created to defame the German people. Stielau's claims had been published in the party's newspaper in December 1958. He saw in *The Diary* a mix of sentimentality and pornographic sexuality aimed at showing the German people in the worst possible light. Stielau charged that the Holocaust, as portrayed in *The Diary*, simply had not happened. The court ordered him dismissed from the civil service and removed from his position in the school system.

But this was in no way the end of the anti-Semites' denial of the reality of *The Diary*. In the United States in 1967 an essay repeating most of the charges made against *The Diary* appeared in what had become a shadow of H. Mencken's *American Mercury*. The author, Teressa Hendry, labeled *The Diary* a "fiction" and dismissed it as part of the libel against the Germans. In 1979, the same year in which Bettelheim published his collection *Surviving*, Ditlieb Felderer published a slim monograph entitled *Anne Frank's Dairy: A Hoax* with the virulently anti-Semitic Institute for Historical Review in California. Felderer presents an interesting case. An Austrian Jew born in 1943, he emigrated to Sweden, where he became a convert to the Jehovah's Witnesses, who sent him to Germany after the war to document the Nazi crimes against their members who were persecuted as pacifists. His pamphlet on *The Diary* is one of the most widely circulated of the revisionist document. Felderer's arguments, while more detailed than the others, are not very different from Stielau's and Hendry's. All were widely reported in the American press. The basis for all their charges was Meyer Levin's lawsuit against Otto Frank and his claim to have written the authentic version of *The Diary*—for the stage! This claim was twisted into a claim that Levin actually wrote *The Diary*: "*The Diary of Anne Frank* . . . has been sold to the public as the actual diary of a young Jewish girl who died in a Nazi concentration camp after two years of abuse and horror . . . Any informed literary inspection of this book would have shown it to have been impossible as the work of a teenager." So says Hendry, but this is the central thesis of all the anti-Semitic readings of *The Diary*. All of these accounts make detailed reference to Levin's court case and interpret the findings of the judge for Levin as "proof" of the fictionality of *The Diary*. Hendry calls *The Diary* fiction labeled as fact. This view is repeated in a widely circulated monograph by Robert Faurisson, the French revisionist, which simply collects the earlier material and arranges it in systematic order. Thus *The Diary* is, for the anti-Semites, further proof of the lying discourse of the Jews. Jews lie, and they lie to profit themselves through the claims of their own annihilation in their creation of "fictions" about themselves. Seen in this light, *The Diary of Anne Frank* is yet another failed Jewish novel. It fails because it is not a "real" representation of the hidden language of the Jews but rather a literary work that any "informed literary inspection" would reveal as a work of fiction written within non-Jewish literary conventions. Thus, part of Levin's unconscious response to the struggle he has with his own Jewish identity is the fact that he has undermined the veracity of *The Diary* as testimony. In claiming to have authored the only valid reading of *The Diary*, he cast the veracity of the diary into doubt. This is Levin's implicit reading, which is then internalized and projected onto everyone involved with the dramatization of the work. It also becomes part of the readings of *The Diary* during the 1960s. What is clear is that the anti-Semitic readings of *The Diary* are but continuations of older charges of the dissimulation of the Jews. Since *The Diary* comes to have a central role in defining the nature of Jewish discourse, the pollution of its interpretation by the anti-Semitic reading causes the figure of Anne Frank to assume a central role in projections of Jewish self-doubt. This is especially the case with *The Diary*'s role in defining the damage discourse of the Jew as a force in shaping the identity of the writer who perceives him- or herself as Jewish.

The confusion surrounding the Jewish readings of *The Diary of Anne Frank* are examined and explained in the work of Philip Roth. Roth's fascination with the double bind situation present within American Jewish identity dominates his writing. Beginning with his collection of short stories, *Goodbye, Columbus* (1959), which won the National Book Award for fiction, Roth comments on the decline of American Jewry under the pressure of the "American way of life." His early ideal for the Jew seems to be the introspective writer *manqué*, like the hero of the title story of that collection, the writer who has yet to prove himself but who separates himself from the commercial world of bourgeois Jewish values. The confusion that reigns among his early characters can best be judged in his tale "Eli, the Fanatic," from *Goodbye, Columbus*. The eponymous hero of the tale confronts the Jew in the form of a group of Eastern European Jews who come to settle in a suburban community. Their dress calls attention to them and thus, in the minds of the local Jews, to the idea of the Jew itself. Eli is sent to persuade the newcomers to change their appearance, their outer sign of identity, which they are quite willing to do. He however, becomes obsessed with the idea of their difference and assumes their cast off garments, becoming a parody of those whose identity as Jews had so frightened and fascinated him.

According to Roth, *Goodbye, Columbus* earned him the label of "being anti-Semitic and 'self-hating,' or at least, tasteless." This attitude was compounded, if anything, when Roth published *Portnoy's Complaint* in 1969. Peter Shaw, the associate editor of the Jewish conservative periodical *Commentary*, concluded his review:

> But if he has not been bad for the Jews, he has decidedly been bad
> to them—and at the expense of his art. For *Portnoy's Complaint*,
> in descending to caricature to get its effects, fails at the very point
> of imagination which raises a novel above a tract. Roth has been
> a positive enemy to his own work, while for the Jews he has been
> a friend of the proverbial sort that makes enemies unnecessary.

Labeled as a "self-hating Jew," a label that arose to characterize the psychopathology of assimilation as represented by the discourse of acculturated Jews, Roth incorporated this charge in his fiction. If the author who writes about Jews in a critical manner is "self-hating," then one manner of dealing with this image is to create a persona, the author labeled as "self-hating Jew," in one's own fiction. Roth begins, in a trilogy about the Jewish American novelist Nathan Zuckerman, to explore the psyche of a Jewish writer identified as writing like a Jew, but a negative Jew, a "bad" Jew, a "self-hating" Jew. Roth explores this psyche, as he had in *Goodbye, Columbus*, with the tools of the social critic, irony and satire. Zuckerman is not Roth or even a Roth surrogate; he is what his readers expect the author of *Portnoy's Complaint* to be. In a sense Roth creates a figure based on the paradigm of the Jew that he rejects: "*Jews are people who are not what anti-Semites say they are. That was once a statement out of which a man might begin to construct an identity for himself; now it does not work so well, for it is difficult to act counter to the ways people expect you to act when fewer and fewer people define you by such expectations.*" Roth wishes to explore how an author labeled "self-hating" arrived at his identity. He reverses the image of the "self-hating" Jew and comes to a definition of the Jews as precisely those people who are not what Jews say they are. He has more than adequate information to construct a "self-hating" identity for Nathan Zuckerman.

Nathan Zuckerman is one of the most complex representations of the Jew as author in modern prose fiction. He first appears in Roth's work as a character in the fiction of Peter Tarnopol, the protagonist of Roth's *My Life as a Man* (1974). Zuckerman is the literary figure whom the author Tarnopol uses to project all of his internalized sense of the "pain of life," having Zuckerman suffer, in the stories, from inexplicable migraines. The use of a character created by a fiction to represent the confusion between life and art, between the charges made in American society about being Jew and a writer and their embodiment within the work of art, raises the problem of self-hatred and its relationship to the "damaged" discourse of the Jew to a new level of analysis. Roth sees the problem as one with the myths of Jewish identity imported from Europe, myths that are inappropriate to the formation of the identity of the American Jew, especially the American Jew as writer. He gives the reader the ultimate confusion between life and art, the confusion that he has his character's character, Zuckerman, experience quite against his logical perception of the world in the course of the trilogy.

The education of Nathan Zuckerman is portrayed in Roth's novel *The Ghost Writer* (1980). In this novel Zuckerman meets the Jewish American short story writer E. I. Lonoff, viewed as a "quaint remnant of the Old World ghetto" whose "fantasies about Americans" some thought "had been written in Yiddish somewhere inside czarist Russia." Lonoff lives as a recluse in New England, married to a woman whose ancestry reaches back to the American Puritans. He divides his time between teaching at a woman's college and drafting and redrafting his "brilliant cycle of comic parables." Lonoff is the Jewish writer as establishment figure. Zuckerman arrives as a newly published author in 1955 to convince Lonoff to "adopt" him as his protégé. In Lonoff's home he meets Amy Bellette, who is ostensibly cataloguing Lonoff's papers for the Harvard Library, where they are to be deposited. A former student of Lonoff's and now his lover, Bellette is revealed in the course of the writer's fantasies to be Anne Frank, who survived the death camps and eventually came to the United States.

The juxtaposition of Anne Frank and Nathan Zuckerman to Lonoff provides Roth with the context in which he defines the Jew as writer. Anne Frank's central position in this definition is heightened by Roth's use of the label "self-hating" for Zuckerman even at this very early stage of his career. Nathan has written a tale of the interfamilial squabbles over the inheritance left by one of his aunts. He sees the story as portraying the strength of character of some of the individuals involved as well as the pettiness of individuals placed in a society without rigid ethical standards. His parents, especially his father, see the story as an attack on all Jews as "moneygrubbing." He sees "himself and all of Jewry gratuitously disgraced and jeopardized by my inexplicable betrayal." His father turns to a remote family acquaintance, a judge who had helped his son get into the University of Chicago, for advice. The judge writes Nathan a long letter, with an appended questionnaire, that points to the potential misuse of his work by a "Julius Streicher or a Joseph Goebbels." The letter ends with a postscript: "If you have not yet seen the Broadway production of *The Diary of Anne Frank*, I strongly advise that you do so. Mrs. Wapter and I were in the audience on opening night; we wish that Nathan Zuckerman could have been with us to benefit from that unforgettable experience." It is the drama based on *The Diary* that defines Anne Frank for this world. It is the image of the speaking, living witness, the dead come to life, the dead never having died, that provides the emotional clue to the inner life of an American Jew as critic. Judge Wapter is the "bad" Jew; he attempts to manipulate Nathan by equating his world with that of Anne Frank, by equating the American Jewish experience after the Holocaust with that of Europe. Roth sees these two worlds as inherently different, separated not only by the difference in the structures of society but by the very occurrence of the Holocaust. In the United States the Holocaust, through its commercialization in works such as the dramatization of *The Diary of Anne Frank*, has provided all Jews with a homogenous history. Roth sees the need to provide autonomy for each individual's experience, to reverse Bruno

Bettelheim's view that the camps were the ultimate loss of autonomy in a mass age. The dramatization of *The Diary* provided a history for all American Jews that was distant from their own private terrors. Zuckerman's father demands that Nathan respond to the judge's letter, but Nathan refuses:

> "Nothing I could write Wapter would convince him of anything. Or his wife."
> "You could tell him you went to see *The Diary of Anne Frank*. You could at least do that."
> "I didn't see it, I read the book. *Everybody* read the book."
> "But you liked it, didn't you?"
> "That's not the issue. How can you *dis*like it? Mother, I will not prate in platitudes to please the adults."

The Diary of Anne Frank is the true experience, the Jew as writer in an appropriate discourse; it is the drama that provides the clue to the middle class's expropriation of fears that are not their own. What happened to the Jews of Europe a decade before the pattern against which Roth's American Jews, those who so freely wield the label of "self-hating Jew" against the writer, measure themselves. But it is a trivial model; it is the world of the commercial theater or film, not the reality of Belsen, that defines their identity. Thus when Roth recounts to Lonoff Amy Bellett's admission that she is Anne Frank (and his seduction by her), it is in terms of the drama. She goes to New York from Boston to see "the dramatization of Anne Frank's diary":

> It wasn't the play—I could have watched that easily enough if I had been alone. It was the people watching with me. Carloads of women kept pulling up to the theater, women wearing fur coats, with expensive shoes and handbags. I thought, This isn't for me. . . . But I showed my ticket, I went in with them, and of course it happened. It had to happen. It's what happens there. The women cried. Everyone around me was in tears. Then at the end, in the row behind me, a woman screamed, "Oh, no." That's why I came running here. . . . And I knew I couldn't when I heard that woman scream "Oh, no." I knew then what's been true all long: . . . I have to be dead to everyone.

It is evident even to Lonoff that she is creating a fiction, indeed a fiction patterned after her mentor's own stories. She recounts her life as Anne Frank, how she survived Belsen as a mute and passive child, how she took the name Bellette from *Little Women* (creating herself as a literary character), how she discovered her father's publication of her diary in an old copy of *Time* in a dentist's office, how she ordered and received a copy of the Dutch original. Roth's reading of *The Diary* through the eyes of Amy Bellette reveals the work as one of unselfconscious self-analysis, but a book that received its force through the writer's death: "But dead she had something more to offer than amusement for ages 10–15; dead she had written, without meaning or trying to, a book with the force of a masterpiece to make people finally see." Roth plays this found work of art off against the craft of the play. And he, too, uses the example of religious celebration. "As for celebrations, she had found St. Nicholas's Day, once she'd been introduced to it in hiding, much more fun than Chanukah, and along with Pim made all kinds of clever gifts and even written a Santa Claus poem to enliven the festivities. . . . How could even the most obtuse of the ordinary ignore what had been done to the Jews *just for being Jews*, how could even the most beknighted of the Gentiles fail to get the idea when they read in *Het Achterhuis* that once a year the Franks sang a harmless Chanukah song, said some Hebrew words, lighted some candles, exchanged some presents—a ceremony lasting some ten minutes—and that was all it took to make them the enemy." Roth makes language, the Hebrew of the liturgy, into the means by which Amy Bellette defines the world of Anne's Jewishness. The "Jewishness" of the drama rings false in Roth's presentation, since it is the most superficial identification with Jewish ritual rather than with Jewish ethics. The Franks' Chanukah, in Roth's eye, is quite parallel to the Jewish wedding presented in the title novella of *Goodbye, Columbus*. It is ritual language without meaning.

It is not simply that Roth sees in the silence imposed on Anne Frank, on her role as the dead author speaking, the misreading of her text. Roth parallels the fate of Lonoff's two "children": Anne, the woman who seduces him, and Nathan, the man who wishes to become his "son." Nathan's upbringing is thus strikingly parallel to that of Anne:

> In fact my own first reading of Lonoff's canon . . . had done more to make me realize how much I was still my family's Jewish offspring than anything I had carried forward to the University of Chicago from childhood Hebrew lessons, or mother's kitchen, or the discussions I used to hear among my parents and our relatives about the perils of intermarriage, the problem of Santa Claus, and the injustice of medical school quotas.

Zuckerman's attraction to Anne, the idea of being "Anne Frank's husband," has some of its roots in his identification with her understanding of herself. Both see themselves as Jews in terms of the minimal identification with the

special language of the Jews—not Hebrew, the language of liturgy, of the
annual visit to the temple, but the Yiddish-tinged language of the Jewish
writer, Lonoff. Lonoff becomes all Jewish writers for Zuckerman. He
becomes (in Zuckerman's analogy) Kafka as well as Babel. And when he
fantasizes Amy into the role of Anne Frank, a role that she created for herself
out of the stuff of Lonoff's fictions and the Hacketts' play, he sees her as
Kafka's "K": "Everything he dreamed in Prague was, to her, real Amsterdam
life. . . . It could be the epigraph for her book. 'Someone must have falsely
traduced Anne F., because one morning without having done anything
wrong, she was placed under arrest.'" Anne is a fiction of Amy in Zuckerman's world. She is a fiction that Zuckerman wishes to use to prove that he
is not a "self-hating" Jew: "Oh, marry me, Anne Frank, exonerate me before
my outraged elders of this idiotic indictment! Heedless of Jewish feeling?
Indifferent to Jewish survival? Brutish about their well-being? Who dares to
accuse of such unthinking crimes the husband of Anne Frank!"

For at this point, at the close of Roth's novel, Zuckerman knows that
Amy is not Anne. "When the sleeve of her coat fell back, I of course saw that
there was no scar on her forearm. No scar; no book; no Pim." Amy's fiction
of Anne Frank enables Zuckerman, the "self-hating" Jew, to perceive that his
voice can be one apart from the fragments of European history that make up
the world of Anne Frank. No scar, no book, only theater. The voice of the
poet, of Lonoff as the master craftsman, is likewise revealed to be dry and
cramped, destructive of art as much as the bourgeois theater in which *The
Diary* is played. Zuckerman can go on to examine that world in which he has
found himself, that world, according to Roth, of social accessibility and
moral indifference, where one cannot always figure out what a Jew is that a
Christian is not.

In Roth's reading of *The Diary of Anne Frank*, the model of self-hatred
incorporated in American consciousness, based on the analogy of the American experience with that of Europe, is drawn into question. Bettelheim,
Steiner, and, indeed, even Meyer Levin accept the polar definition of the
"self-hating" Jew, one who internalizes the charges of anti-Semitic rhetoric,
specifically about the nature of his own language, and projects these charges
onto others labeled as Jews. For Bettelheim the villain is Otto Frank; Levin
sees in him the same villain, the "bad" Jew, but for quite different reasons.
Roth takes the idea of the Jewish writer in post-Holocaust American society
as his theme. He wishes to examine how the very process of internalization
and projection works in forming the consciousness and identity of his proto-
typical "Jewish" writer, Nathan Zuckerman. Roth's point of departure is his
fictionalization of the double bind in which writers such as Bettelheim,
Steiner, Adorno, and Levin found themselves when "reading" *The Diary of*

Anne Frank. They saw the work, especially when presented as a play or a movie, as a resuscitation of the Jew as victim, without acknowledging that such an action would draw into question the very role of the survivor. This double bind situation, the survivor's confrontation with the survival of the victim, a victim seemingly better able than the survivor-witness to articulate the horror of the Holocaust, becomes the stuff of Roth's fiction. In the education of Nathan Zuckerman, in his confrontation and fantasy about Anne Frank, is the very stuff of the double bind of contemporary readings of *The Diary of Anne Frank*, distanced through the use of satire and understood as part of the European inheritance that shapes the identity of the American Jewish writer. Roth wishes to distance himself from the world of Nathan Zuckerman, from the world of the Jew who internalizes the charge of the silence of the Jew as victim and the special role assigned to the articulate Jew as witness, the Jewish author as the creator of his own undamaged discourse. In the various readings of *The Diary of Anne Frank* one can see the function of such a text, especially in its form as play and movie, in providing the matrix for a discussion of the appropriate language of the Jew as survivor.

SYLVIA PATTERSON ISKANDER

Anne Frank's Reading

Anne Frank's *Diary of a Young Girl* unfolds the story of a sensitive teenager in the throes of transition to womanhood, reveals an intimate portrait of eight people hiding in Amsterdam during World War II, fearful for their very lives, and offers a glimpse of some sincere, faithful Dutch men and women willing to risk their lives to aid their Jewish friends living in what Anne called *het achterhuis* or the "secret annex."

Miep Gies (pseudonym Miep Van Santen), perhaps the greatest source of comfort, supplies, and business assistance to the group in hiding had the foresight to save the orange plaid–covered diary and Anne's later papers, a revision of her work with an eye to publication, all of which were tossed in disarray from Mr. Frank's briefcase on that fateful day of 4 August 1944 when the Green Police stormed into the annex, removed the occupants, and confiscated everything they believe to be of value. Miep's own account, published in 1986, of those war-torn years when death and starvation were the norm, complements Anne's diary and in a sense completes the unfinished journal. Miep tells of gathering the diary, storing it unread in her desk, hoping to return it to Anne one day, and of her husband Henk retrieving the library books, among others, from the annex the day their friends were arrested. Miep later presented the diary to Mr. Frank, the only survivor from the secret annex. Concerned for his daughter's memory and the privacy of

From *Children's Literature Association Quarterly* 13:3 (Fall 1988). © 1988 by Southwest Texas State University.

others still living, Frank at first refused to publish the manuscript, but later reversed his decision when friends prevailed upon him because of the uniqueness of its account of the war from the perspective of a young girl. The *Diary* soon became a great success. Upon his death in 1980, Otto Frank willed all his daughter's papers to the Dutch National Institute for War Documentation.

The complete, unexpurgated *Diary*, now available in Dutch, will be published in English for the first time by Doubleday in [June 1989]. Undoubtedly, it will reveal more of Anneliese Marie Frank's autobiographical talent, a product of her education and learning experiences which resulted in large measure from her reading, both for recreational and for study purposes. I have used both versions currently available to trace Anne's reading, as well as *Brinkman's Catalogue* to verify which books or editions were in print in Holland prior to 1945.

On 11 July 1943, almost a year to the day after the family entered their hiding place in the unused laboratory and storehouse of Mr. Frank's office, Anne writes to Kitty, her fictional diary correspondent: "Ordinary people simply don't know what books mean to us, shut up here. Reading, learning, and the radio are our amusements." Reading relieved the long hours of silence imposed on the Franks, the Van Daans, and Mr. Dussel for fear of being overheard by employees carrying on their daily business in the front of the house on the Prinsengracht Canal. Since the group frequently read the same books, they could discuss them in the evenings and late afternoons when, according to Anne, they "pass the time in all sorts of crazy ways: asking riddles, physical training in the dark, talking English and French, criticizing books." Anne often discusses books with sixteen year old Peter Van Daan in their solitary talks in the attic room, and Otto Frank frequently reads aloud to the children from Dickens and from plays by Goethe and Schiller, such as *Don Carlos*. Mr. Frank's emphasis on books is attested to by his request that Anne and her sister, Margot, keep a card file of titles and authors of books which they read.

Anne compares the residents of the secret annex to little children receiving a present when new books arrive on Saturdays, brought by friends and employees of Mr. Frank's firm, for whom Anne invented the pseudonyms of Mr. Koophuis, Mr. Kraler, and Miep and Henk Van Santen. Some books are gifts for birthdays and other holidays; others are loaned from the library or from friends. Occasionally, a library due date challenges Anne to complete a book (11 May 1944). Once, 10 August 1943, a forbidden book incites Anne's criticism of Dussel for "indirectly endangering our lives" because Miep obtains a book for him "which abuses Mussolini and Hitler."

Annuals, magazines, and newspapers are welcome gifts. On 11 July 1942, Mr. Koophuis presents Anne with the *Young People's Annual*, containing fairy tales, stories, and poems by such writers as Hans Christian Andersen, the Brothers Grimm, Jack London, Jules Verne, and H. G. Wells. Anne loves to read *Cinema and Theater*, a movie magazine which Mr. Kraler delivers on Mondays, enabling her to keep current with the latest films and stars. The collection of cut-out photographs hanging on the walls of her small room, measuring approximately 7 feet by 16 feet, reflects her interest in such famous people as Deanna Durbin, Robert Stack, Rudy Vallee, Norma Shearer, Greta Garbo, Ray Milland, Ginger Rogers, and even skating great Sonji Henie. Other visitors to the hiding place, such as Mr. Koophuis and Henk, bring newspapers and books which they discuss with the young people (28 January 1944). Anne even dreams about a book, one of drawings by Mary Bos (6 January 1944), the only author not identified in this study.

One article Anne discusses just with Kitty, not visitors, however, is about blushing by Sis Heyster, who authored several books on child and adolescent psychology. Anne believes the article might have been addressed to her personally, for its discussion of pubescent girls' feelings coincides with her experiences (5 January 1944). Her strong emotions about certain books elicit the comment of 8 November 1943, "If I read a book that impresses me, I have to take myself firmly in hand, before I mix with other people; otherwise they would think my mind rather queer." Her frequent identification with books she reads can have negative results as well. For example, her dislike of math makes her algebra text her most loathed book; when a vase breaks, spilling water over her books and papers on 20 May 1944, she is disappointed that the algebra book is not ruined and threatens its destruction: "If I'm ever in a really very wicked mood, I'll tear the blasted thing to pieces!"

In addition to algebra, Anne studies under Otto Frank's tutelage languages, history, science, religion, art, and geography. She frequently refers to *Koenen*, a Dutch dictionary. Relating her program of study for a single day, 27 April 1944, she states:

> First, I translated a piece from Dutch into English about Nelson's last battle. After that, I went through some more of Peter the Great's war against Norway (1700–1721), Charles XII, Augustus the Strong, Stanislavs Leczinsky, Mazeppa, Von Görz, Brandenburg, Pomerania and Denmark, plus the usual dates.
>
> After that I landed up in Brazil, read about Bahia tobacco, the abundance of coffee and the one and a half million inhabitants of Rio de Janeiro, of Pernambuco and Sao Paulo, not forgetting the river Amazon; about Negroes, Mulattos, Mestizos, Whites, more than fifty percent of the population being illiterate, and the

malaria. As there was still some time left, I quickly ran through a family tree. Jan the elder, Willem Lodewijk, Ernst Casimir I, Hendrik Casimir I, . . . Margriet Franciska (born in 1943 in Ottawa).

Twelve o'clock: In the attic, I continued my program with the history of the Church—Phew! Till one o'clock.

Just after two, the poor child sat working ('hm,'hm!) again, this time studying narrow- and broad-nosed monkeys. Kitty, tell me quickly how many toes a hippopotamus has! Then followed the Bible, Noah and the Ark, Shem, Ham, and Japheth. After that Charles V. Then with Peter: *The Colonel*, in English, by Thackeray. Heard my French verbs and then compared the Mississippi with the Missouri.

Under this program of study, Anne advances rapidly, yet the Franks maintain that Margot is the real student of the family.

In conjunction with her study of French and English, Anne keeps a notebook for foreign words and reads in French Alphonse Daudet's delightful *La Belle Nivernaise: Histoire d'un vieux bateau et son equipage* and in English Oscar Wilde's four-act comedy *The Ideal Husband*, as well as the book by Thackeray mentioned above, which perhaps may be *The History of Henry Esmond, Esq.: A Colonel in the Service of Her Majesty Queen Anne*.

Clearly Anne learns much history, music, and science from reading biographies such as *Emperor Charles V*, which took Professor Karl Brandi forty years to write, *Maria Theresa* by Karl Tschuppik, who also wrote biographies on Franz Joseph and Elizabeth of Austria, *Hungarian Rhapsody*, the life of Franz Liszt by Zsolt Harsányi, who authored as well a biography of Galileo Galilei, and perhaps Knut Hagberg's *Carl Linnaeus*, a book Mr. Frank received for his birthday on 12 May 1944 from Koophuis, which Anne may not have read. She does read contemporary history, however, such as *Palestine at the Crossroads*, and her strong interest in the genealogy of many royal families evokes the reference to genealogy on 6 April 1944 as her number two hobby (number one being writing); this interest, furthered by her reading in biography and history, is attested to by her copying the long genealogical tables found in *Emperor Charles V* and by her posting on her bedroom wall pictures of the youthful Princesses Elizabeth and Margaret Rose. She even states on 21 April 1944, her wish that Margaret might marry Prince Baudouin of Belgium.

Another of Anne's interests, religion, apparently increases with time. On 29 October 1942, Mrs. Frank gives her prayer book in German to Anne to read, but the prayers do not have much meaning for Anne. A year later, her father requests a copy of a children's Bible from Mr. Koophuis so that she can learn about the New Testament. When Margot asks on 3 November 1943 if Anne will receive the book for Chanukah, Mr. Frank suggests St. Nicholas's Day as more appropriate. Although Anne clearly recognizes her Jewish heritage and daily confronts the problems of being Jewish in Hitler's reign of terror, she also posts on her wall a picture of Jesus from Michelangelo's famous *Pietà*.

Her fondness for art, perhaps accounting for the *Pietà* picture and a copy of Rembrandt's *Portrait of an Old Man* on her wall is strengthened by the gift of Anton Springer's five-volume *History of Art* for Anne's fifteenth birthday.

Vivid illustrations enhance *Tales and Legends of the Netherlands* by Joseph Cohen, a book Anne receives for her thirteenth birthday along with money with which she hopes to purchase *The Myths of Greece and Rome* by H. A. Guerber, who collected myths about the Norsemen and the Middle Ages as well. Anne's interest in mythology, hobby number four and not a part of her regular program of study, is confirmed by a picture of an unidentified Greek god in her room and sparked by Guerber's book, which she does not purchase, but instead receives on her fourteenth birthday.

The Franks obviously oversee their children's reading, occasionally restricting it. On 2 September 1942, Anne says, "Margot and Peter can read nearly all the books Mr. Koophuis lends us," but they are forbidden to read a certain book (unnamed) about women. Peter's quite normal curiosity urges him to disobey and continue reading the book until he is caught by his parents and punished. Margot is allowed to read one book, forbidden to Anne because of her younger age (21 September 1942): *Heeren, knechten en vrouwen*, or *Gentlemen, Servants and Women*. In this first book of a trilogy about a *burgemeester* or mayor of Amsterdam and his family, the mayor considers betraying his country's alliance with England by assisting the French in sending arms to the American colonies in their fight for independence. Whether the issues of patriotism and betrayal, or sexual issues which also appear, or all of them made the Franks censor the book for their thirteen year old is impossible to say. To the Franks' credit, however, is the fact that a year and a half later on 17 March 1944, Anne reveals that although all books she reads are "inspected," her parents "are not at all strict, and I'm allowed to read nearly everything."

Three books mentioned in the *Diary* (13 May 1944) not expressly forbidden to Anne, but which she may not have read are Arend Tael's *Little Martin*, a birthday gift to Dussel from Kraler; a nature book (title and author not stated), a gift to Otto Frank from Kraler; and Gerhard Werkman's *Amsterdam by the Water*, a book containing numerous photographs of the waterways of Amsterdam, some depicting such sports activities as swimming, boating, and fishing.

Other adult fiction which Anne reads are Eric Lowe's *Cloudless Morn*, the first in a trilogy on the *History of Robin Stuart*, a book everyone in the annex enjoys (12 January 1944) and Mrs. Frank particularly likes because of its presentation of the problems of youth; and Ina Boudier-Bakker's *The Knock at the Door*, a story of four generations from 1860 to 1920, including philosophical ideas prevalent at the time. Anne's mixed emotions about the latter are reflected in her comments of 12 March 1943 when she first says that she cannot "drag herself away from [it]," and then reveals that the "story of the family is exceptionally well-written. Apart from that, it is about war, writers, the emancipation of women; and quite honestly I'm not awfully interested."

Contrasting with the textbooks and adult works are those which might be classified as young-adult fiction: Niklaus Bolt's *Daisy's Mountain Holiday*, described by Anne as "terrific" when she received it for her thirteenth birthday; Nico van Suchtelen's *Eva's Youth*, a romantic story about the youth of a small girl Eva, whose monthly period is discussed and which is perhaps the source of Anne's forthright discussion of hers (29 October 1942); Helene Haluschka's *What Do You think of the Modern Young Girl?*, a library book criticizing the youth of the time and evoking one of Anne's most insightful discussions about herself, her relationship with her parents and with Peter Van Daan, and finally her belief in the goodness of people and her hope for peace and tranquility (15 July 1944); and last, Marianne Philip's *Henry from the Other Side*, a book Dussel likes enough to recommend, but then criticizes Anne's dislike of it by complaining (29 July 1943) that she cannot "understand the psychology of a man!" Although this book and others ostensibly appear to be the source of arguments, in reality the source is the inevitable tension resulting from such differing personality types in extremely close quarters over an extended period of time.

No one argued, however, with Anne about her favorite author, Cissy van Marxveldt, a prolific writer who composed in Anne's lifetime four of the five books in the *Joop ter Heul* series, still popular in Holland. The series about a young girl growing to maturity with a most unusual name for a female "thrilled" Anne when she read it in September and October of 1942, and she claims that she enjoyed "very much" all of van Marxveldt's works, having read *Een Zomerzotheid*, roughly translated as *Summer Antics*, four times. She did not like *De Stormes* (*The Assault*) as well as the Joop series, but refers to the young-adult author not only as "first-rate," but also as one whom she will let her own children read one day. The fun-loving Joop, who corresponds with her friend Net until her father limits her letter writing and she turns to keeping a diary, also has a friend named Kitty, perhaps Anne's inspiration for her imaginary correspondent.

These then are the twenty-six books, two plays, one article, and one magazine specifically named in the *Diary*. The importance of reading cannot be overstated, for the role it played in the education, as well as the recreation of Anne and the others. Mr. Frank should be credited not only with a most appropriate selection of birthday gifts for his daughters, but also, and more importantly, with encouraging them to read, discuss, and think critically. Surprisingly, almost all the books they read were at the time very recent publications. Authored by writers from Germany, England, France, Sweden, Australia, Hungary, Switzerland, as well as The Netherlands, they represent a wide diversity and a broad spectrum and reflect Anne's reading in Dutch, German, French, and English. Perhaps they contributed to her tolerance for others and her hope for the future in the midst of undeniable fear and horror, for Anne wished to publish her diary to achieve her desire for peace, as well as her longing for fame as a writer.

The untimely death of Anne Frank from typhus at Bergen-Belsen Concentration Camp just two months prior to the end of the war adds a poignancy to the *Diary*, whose universality is confirmed by the sale of more than fifteen million copies and by its translation into more than fifty languages. Exhibitions, plays, films, even art work attest to the success of this youthful writer, who certainly has achieved her desire for fame, although not yet her desire for peace in the world.

Editor's Note: Both "Anne Frank's Reading" and Sylvia Patterson Iskander's essay that follows, "Anne Frank's Autobiographical Style," were written prior to publication of the unexpurgated version of the diary. A revision and enlargement of "Anne Frank's Reading" is currently being edited and prepared by Professor Hyman Enzer of Hofstra University.

—H. B.

SYLVIA PATTERSON ISKANDER

Anne Frank's Autobiographical Style

Anne Frank's *Diary of a Young Girl*, originally entitled *Het Achterhuis* (*The Secret Annex*), presents a self portrait that captivates most readers initially because of their foreknowledge of the tragic conclusion of this young girl's life and the other horrors of the Holocaust. Subsequently, Anne's revelation of her unique personality and her unusual circumstances rivet readers to the *Diary*, proclaiming it a classic. An examination of Anne's writing techniques reveals, in addition, a thoroughly professional style, which also contributes significantly to the book's merit. Anne's style, in fact, is so unusual for a thirteen to fifteen-year-old that her authorship has been questioned. Extensive handwriting analysis, however, has verified the *Diary's* authenticity. Although sometimes censored for its politics or ideology, its attitude toward adults, and its revelation of sexual maturation, the *Diary*, if excised only slightly as Otto Frank, Anne's father, has indicated and if accurately translated, is an achievement of rare and precious worth.

The complete, unexpurgated *Diary*, now available in Dutch, appeared in English for the first time published by Doubleday in June, 1989. I believe that it reveals more of her autobiographical talent, for Anneliese Marie Frank employed many and varied techniques, some acquired, no doubt, from her own reading. Under her father's tutelage, Anne studied several excellent histories and biographies, which probably influenced her style; she specifically

From *Children's Literature Association Quarterly* 16:2 (Summer 1991). © 1991 by Southwest Texas State University.

mentions in the *Dairy*: Karl Brandi's *The Emperor Charles V*, Zsolt Harsányi's biographies of Galileo and Franz Liszt, Karl Tschuppik's *Maria Theresa*, and others. Her reading—of books originally published in English, German, French, Hungarian, Swedish, as well as Dutch, of myths and legends, popular young-adult novels, articles on psychology, movie and theater magazines, a young people's annual, plays, and even the Bible—impressed Anne, whose assimilation of them with her own intuition enabled her to create her remarkable journalistic style.

Anne cannot be compared as a theorist to the eighteenth-century English masters of biography and autobiography, Samuel Johnson and James Boswell, whose innovations in the field established the still-current criteria, but she actually utilized most of their theories about style, perhaps absorbing them from the biographies that she read. Whether she developed her style on her own or from her reading of European writers following in the Johnson/Boswell tradition, we may never know. One possible explanation, however, is that she absorbed much of this tradition through her reading of Professor Brandi's biography of Emperor Charles V, over which he labored forty years while at Göttingen University in Germany. Göttingen, founded by George II of England and Hanover in 1734, certainly contained by the early twentieth century, most of Johnson's and Boswell's works, for its collection has long been noted for its rich English holdings. Brandi emulates Johnson's ideas in including not just the significant events, but also the minutiae of his subject's daily life; his stated goal is to paint not a hero's portrait, but a man's with frailties and virtues.

Anne also emulates the eighteenth-century biographers in various ways; her introspective method, for one, reveals her ability to view herself as an outsider, her awareness of a prospective audience, her desire to be a writer, and her abundant possession of the autobiographer's primary prerequisite: knowledge of self. Though sometimes confused by her own conflicting emotions, typical of the teen years, she possesses a relentless interest, curiosity, and objectivity which provoke her to examine her own activities and thoughts intimately, an examination which places her diary among the best of this century's with the distinction of being the most translated Dutch books.

Although Anne "assimilate[s] external events" such as news of the war, in the *Diary*, her most unusual characteristic is her ability to view life as an outsider; for example, she speaks of her younger self on 7 March 1944, as "a different Anne who has grown wise within these walls"; she says, "that Anne [was] an amusing, but very superficial girl, who has nothing to do with the Anne of today"; and she continues, "I look upon my life up till the New Year, as it were, through a powerful magnifying glass." Her introspection is evident also on 7 May 1944, when she has been chastised by her father; she comments, "It's right that for once I've been taken down from my inaccessible pedestal, that my pride has been shaken a bit, for I was becoming much too taken up with myself again. What Miss Anne does is by no means always right!" This young woman admits to knowing her own faults (14 June 1944) "better than anyone, [she says] but the difference is that I also know that I want to improve, shall improve, and have already improved a great deal." This statement is perhaps self-justification, perhaps a sincere attempt to present herself in a better light for the implied reader.

Doubtless Anne had a view of posterity reading her diary. On 29 July 1943, she writes a postscript to her journal entry, "Will the reader take into consideration that when this story was written [about Mrs. Van Daan's bad qualities] the writer had not cooled down from her fury!" Her awareness of potential readers is again divulged when she cross-references a dream about Peter Wessel. In the 28 April 1944 entry, she urges herself or the implied reader to see "the beginning of January" for her first account of the dream. Further, her creation of Kitty, a stylistic stroke of genius, was influenced, I believe, by the epistolary style in the first book of Cissy van Marxveldt's *Joop ter Heul* series; Anne says on 20 June 1942, "I want this diary to be my friend, and I shall call my friend Kitty." Joop, in the opening book of van Marxveldt's still popular series of adolescent novels, also writes to a fictitious friend "Net," and another in her school club is named "Kitty." Anne's imaginary correspondent is more than just a name for her diary; this "friend" presumably is a pseudo-interviewer; for example, the 6 April 1944 entry commences with this address to Kitty: "You asked me what my hobbies and interests were, so I want to reply." Later she suggest to "Kits" that her diary with all its nonsense should be entitled "The unbosomings of an ugly duckling." Regardless of title, Anne's awareness of audience extended even to a desire to publish her diary after the war. The version, unexpurgated by her father, from which a few excerpts were published in English prior to 1989 reveal Anne's adherence to Johnson's and Boswell's repugnance for panegyric in biography. Otto Frank, perhaps not less aware than Anne of the audience's need for absolute truth in autobiography, was, however, more aware of the invasion of privacy of persons still living.

Anne incorporates many other autobiographical techniques expounded by Samuel Johnson and aptly illustrated by James Boswell. She not only adheres to Johnson's dictum that the autobiographer is the best biographer because he possesses knowledge of self, but also her diary provides evidence of Johnson's beliefs as stated in *The Rambler*, No. 60, that any man is a fit subject for biography, that no detail is too minute to be included, and that biography should be didactic. To these dicta in his immortal *Life of Johnson*,

Boswell added the results of his own phenomenal memory, his ability at recreating conversation and depicting dramatic scenes, his strong sense of personal pride, and his great confidence in his writing ability.

All of these qualities and characteristics describe Anne as well. Her knowledge of self is evident to herself and to others as she questions her identity, like all teens, when she ponders her attractiveness to boys, her writing ability, and even her chances for surviving the war. No detail is too small for inclusion; for example, Anne's reading of Nico van Suchtelen's tale of a young girl from a small town, entitled *Eva's Youth*, in which Eva's monthly period is openly discussed may have been the impetus for her frank revelations about her budding sexuality. Anne enumerates other details, such as her birthday gifts, the food eaten on numerous occasions, even the order of the bathroom queue. In regard to the didactic purpose of autobiography, Anne's strong desire for peace and freedom evince in the reader a profound sense of injustice for Anne and the members of the Annex and a sense of horror for the atrocities of the Holocaust; the moral lessons are evident to the reader, even though Anne may not always have been conscious of them as she wrote.

Like Boswell, Anne recreates actual or at least typical conversations, sets dramatic scenes, and describes the various personalities in the Annex trying to live together harmoniously, such as the following brief but discerning description, which she labels, "the views of the five grownups":

> Mrs. Van Daan: "This job as queen of the kitchen lost its attraction a long time ago. It's dull to sit and do nothing, so I go back to my cooking again. . . . Nothing but ingratitude and rude remarks do I get in return for my services. I am always the black sheep, always the guilty one. Moreover, according to me, very little progress is being made in the war; in the end the Germans will still win. I'm afraid we're going to starve, and if I'm in a bad mood I scold everyone."
>
> Mr. Van Daan: "I must smoke and smoke and smoke, and then the food, the political situation, and Keril's moods don't seem so bad. Keril is a darling wife. . . ."
>
> Mrs. Frank: "Food is not very important, but I would love a slice of rye bread now, I feel so terribly hungry. If I were Mrs. Van Daan I would have put a stop to Mr. Van Daan's everlasting smoking a long time ago. But now I must definitely have a cigarette, because my nerves are getting the better of me. The English make a lot of mistakes, but still the war is progressing. I must have a chat and be thankful I'm not in Poland."

> Mr. Frank: "Everything's all right. I don't require anything.
> Take it easy, we've ample time. Give me my potatoes and then I
> will keep my mouth shut. Put some of my rations on one side for
> Elli. The political situation is very promising. I'm extremely
> optimistic!"
>
> Mr. Dussel: "I must get my task for today, everything must be
> finished on time. Political situation 'outschtänding' and it is
> 'eempossible' that we'll be caught."

These thumbnail sketches describing the five adults in the Annex are a
tribute to Anne's ability to capture in a few lines the essence of the characters with their differing and conflicting personalities.

In contrast, another scene depicts the kind-hearted Peter and the realistic Anne in a conversation typical of teenagers everywhere, interesting
because it lacks the sophistication of the earlier description. Anne's writing
style here matches the girl herself as she faces her boyfriend: immature,
somewhat argumentative, a bit unsure:

> Peter so often used to say, "Do laugh, Anne!" This struck me
> as odd, and I asked, "Why must I always laugh?"
>
> "Because I like it; you get such dimples in your cheeks when
> you laugh; how do they come, actually?"
>
> "I was born with them. I've got one in my chin too. That's my
> only beauty!"
>
> "Of course not, that's not true."
>
> "Yes, it is, I know quite well that I'm not a beauty; I never
> have been and never shall be."
>
> "I don't agree at all, I think you're pretty."
>
> "That's not true."
>
> "If I say so, then you can take it from me it is."

Anne exhibits a lack of confidence in her beauty when flirting with
Peter and in her fear that she will never achieve her life-long dream to go to
Hollywood; yet she exhibits a strong sense of confidence in her writing
ability and her critical faculties. She says on 4 April 1944: "I know that I can
write, a couple of my stories are good, my descriptions of the 'Secret Annexe'
are humorous, there's a lot in my diary that speaks, but—whether I have real
talent remains to be seen. . . . I am the best and sharpest critic of my own
work. I know myself what is and what is not well written. . . . I want to go on
living even after my death! And therefore I am grateful to God for giving me
this gift, this possibility of developing myself and of writing, of expressing all

that is in me . . . [W]ill I ever be able to write anything great, will I ever become a journalist or a writer? I hope so, oh, I hope so very much." Her self-criticism and her desire for publication, perhaps encouraged by Dutch Minister Bolkesteim's appeal on 28 March 1944 over Radio Orange (the Dutch government's radio exiled to London) for diaries and letters written during the war, may have been the impetus for her to begin revising the *Diary* for later publication; these revisions on single sheets of paper, rather than the orange plaid diary proper, formed the basis for the first publication.

Other techniques Anne employed are, to coin Samuel Richardson's phrase, "writing to the moment," creating a sense of immediacy; for example, she apologizes to Kitty saying "that my style is not up to standard today. I have just written down what came into my head." She skips days even up to a month if nothing eventful happens, showing her selectivity of detail; she tells Kitty, "I have deserted you for a whole month, but honestly, there is so little news here that I can't find amusing things to tell every day," a statement that also reveals her awareness of potential audience.

Anne's presentation of a typical day in her life suggest her objectivity and her awareness of an overall view of life in the Annex; her descriptions of people, such as Peter, events, ideas, fears, hopes, reveal the best in Anne's style. She says of Peter, "When he lies with his head on his arm with his eyes closed, then he is still a child; when he plays with Boche [the cat], he is loving; when he carries potatoes or anything heavy, then he is strong; when he goes and watches the shooting, or looks for burglars in the darkness, then he is brave; and when he is so awkward and clumsy, then he is just a pet." Anne's ability to summarize salient points, such as the rules for Jews in Amsterdam, the rules under which the group in the Secret Annex lived, or even the summary of Anne's life itself about six months before she was arrested by the Green Police and taken to Westerbork, Auschwitz, and finally Bergen-Belsen, is proof of her objectivity, both toward herself and others.

These stylistic techniques, coupled with the poignancy of the death of such a talented young fifteen-year-old girl and the horrors of the Holocaust, have justified the sale of over fifteen million copies, the book's translation into more than fifty languages, the play, film, and ballet based on the *Diary*, the Chagall lithograph and Pieter d'Hont statue, the 1978 exhibition in Japan and the exhibition "Anne Frank in the World, 1929–1945," which toured the United States in the late 1980s, the conversion of the home in Amsterdam to the Anne Frank Museum with its half a million visitors annually, the establishment of the Anne Frank Foundation in the Netherlands with its New York branch, the publication of Anne's other writings in a collection entitled *Tales from the Secret Annex*, and, last but not least, the enduring interest in Anne Frank and her writing.

MOLLY MAGID HOAGLAND

Anne Frank On and Off Broadway

"Everything that one says about the play, one says about Anne Frank," wrote the *New York Times* critic Brooks Atkinson 40 years ago. He was talking about *The Diary of Anne Frank*, a stilted, sentimental drama by the Hollywood veterans Frances Goodrich and Albert Hackett that had a triumphant run on Broadway in 1955–56. Now there is a Broadway revival of the play, enjoying a similar if more muted success, and based on a new and allegedly more faithful edition of Anne's diary than the one available in the early 50's.

The new *Diary of Anne Frank* will surely inspire a rash of fresh productions from coast to coast. This is regrettable; for, contrary to Brooks Atkinson, what one says about the play—whether the play of 1955 or the play of 1997—has little to do with the Anne Frank that emerges from her diary.

Anne Frank began keeping a diary on June 12, 1942, her cheerful thirteenth birthday. Three weeks later, she went into hiding with her parents, Otto and Edith, and her sister, Margot, in a garret above the fruit-pectin and spice factory her father had founded in Amsterdam after fleeing Germany in 1933. The Franks were joined by Otto's business partner, Hermann van Pels; his wife and son; and later by an acquaintance, Fritz Pfeffer. They called their hiding place *Het Achterhuis:* in English translation, the "house behind," or "secret annex."

From *Commentary* 105:3 (March 1998). © 1998 by *Commentary.* Reprinted with permission; all rights reserved.

Anne's diary, originally begun as a record of schoolgirl gossip, became, in hiding, an intellectual and spiritual lifeline—the more so after March 1944, when the Dutch government-in-exile broadcast a call for reports of endurance in wartime. "Of course, everyone [in the secret annex] pounced on my diary," the fourteen-year-old Anne wrote the next day. With literary precocity she set about reworking her previous entries while simultaneously writing new ones. She created pseudonyms for the eight in hiding, and the five Dutch friends who sustained them. The van Pelses became the "van Daans," Fritz Pfeffer "Albert Dussel"; so they have been known ever since. She also started to plan a novel based on the diary: "People would find it very amusing to read how we lived, what we ate, and what we talked about as Jews in hiding."

Anne's diary came to an abrupt close on August 1, 1944, three days before the eight Jews were betrayed by an unknown person and seized in their hiding place. They were deported to the Westerbork camp in northern Holland, then to Auschwitz and elsewhere. In February or March 1945, Anne died of typhus in Bergen-Belsen, following her sister Margot by just days. Alone of the group, Otto Frank survived the war, was liberated from Auschwitz, and returned to Amsterdam.

Immediately after the eight had been arrested, their devoted helper Miep Gies retrieved Anne's writings from the annex and hid them, unread, through the war. These she gave to Otto Frank in the summer of 1945, the day they learned Anne Frank was indeed dead. After a time Otto showed portions of the diary to friends in Amsterdam; stunned by its eloquence, they encouraged him to find a publisher. In 1947, a Dutch edition was brought out, and French and West German versions appeared three years later. In 1952, the New York firm of Doubleday published *Anne Frank: The Diary of a Young Girl*; its unexpected success led to publication in more than twenty countries.

This version of the diary is what was adapted for the stage by the married team of Goodrich and Hackett, their quiet collaborator Lillian Hellman, and the director Garson Kanin. (The Hacketts also produced a film version in 1959.) But the Anne Frank presented on Broadway was a construct. As many critics have since pointed out, missing from the play were Anne's intellect, her sense of irony, her dark foreboding, her sensuality, and most of all her Jewish consciousness. What was left were, in Brooks Atkinson's enthusiastic words, "the bloom of her adolescence" and her challenge to "the conscience of the world," which unfortunately amounted to little more than a pallid universalism.

The sorry tale of the diary's dramatization has been exposed recently (though to different ends) by Lawrence Graver in *An Obsession with Anne*

Frank (1995) and Ralph Melnick in *The Stolen Legacy of Anne Frank* (1997). Melnick reserves special scorn for Otto Frank, who had a weakness for people claiming to admire his daughter and, more importantly who saw Anne, in his own words, as "an adolescent believing in the future," an ecumenical "symbol for the whole world." Although late in the process Otto developed misgivings about the play's fidelity to the diary, by that time the production was no longer legally bound to him and he was left to defer to the Hacketts' and Kanin's theatrical expertise. It was, after all, on the basis of that expertise that Otto had justified his choice of them over the writer Meyer Levin.

Levin, an ardent Zionist and the author of the best-selling novel *Compulsion* (about the 1924 Leopold-Loeb murder case in Chicago), had read the diary in French before its American appearance; had promoted it with a rave review in the *New York Times*; had originated the idea of dramatizing it; had worked to that end as an unpaid literary agent; and had written a stage adaptation that was more faithful, and much more Jewish, than the Hacketts'. When Otto Frank rejected both Levin and his play, the writer entered into a decades-long fixation, of which his protracted lawsuit against Frank was only one expression.

As Lawrence Graver shows in his enlightening literary and psychological study, Levin could be an irrational bully, both destructive and self-destructive. (His own account of the affair, *The Obsession*, published in 1973, offers ample evidence on both scores.) Essentially, though, the pugnacious Levin attacked Otto Frank on the same grounds as have Frank's present-day detractors, if with greater heat. He accused Frank, whom he characterized as a timid assimilationist, of "censoring" and "betraying" Anne's words, and in particular of suppressing both Anne and Levin himself as "too Jewish." More, Levin constructed an overwrought self-identification with Anne as a fellow persecuted writer. To her he wrote an eighteen-page posthumous letter entitle "Another Way to Kill a Writer"; to Otto, a note stating, "You have been my Hitler."

Levin, though paranoid, did have enemies, and Melnick, a Levin partisan, demonstrates that he was right to feel aggrieved. For there was a concerted effort, by Hellman and the others, to banish Levin from the dramatization, and also to dilute its Jewish content. Graver attributes the playing-down of Anne's Jewishness to box-office worries, particularly on the part of the director Garson Kanin. As for Levin's suspicion that radical left-wing impulses were also at work—he claimed that Lillian Hellman was leading the campaign to "universalize" the play's message in order to make it into a vehicle of Communist propaganda—this Graver blames on the conspiratorial atmosphere of the McCarthy years. In retrospect, both elements seem to have been present, though Graver passes too easily over

Hellman's indisputably ideological agenda, while Melnick, for his part, assigns it too much weight.

In the Hacketts' play, at any rate, perhaps the most egregious piece of optimistic "universalizing" occurs in the final scene between Anne and the young Peter van Daan, shortly before the Nazis descend on the group. At Kanin's insistence, Anne's repeated reflections on Jewish suffering in the diary were transformed into a gushing sentiment whose crowning thought rings particularly false:

> "We're not the only people that've had to suffer. There've always been people that've had to . . . sometimes one race . . . sometimes another. . . . I still believe, in spite of everything, that people are really good at heart." Here Anne and Peter stand hand in hand until the screeching of the vehicles coming to arrest them is heard outside.

The production now on Broadway, though still the Hacketts' play, has been adapted by Wendy Kesselman in a manner clearly designed to repair its faults. In fact, the revival was prompted by the publication in 1995 of a definitive edition of the diary that advertised itself as restoring "passages originally withheld by [Anne's] father." Drawn by the allure of this once-"censored" text, Kesselman and the play's director, James Lapine, set out to portray the "unexpurgated" Anne: a more intellectual, more political, more sexual, and more Jewish young woman who (as they told the *New York Times*) "listened to clandestine radio broadcasts and understood that the Nazis were gassing Jews." Toward this end, Kesselman has both reworked a number of elements in the Hacketts' script and inserted excerpts from the new edition of the diary.

The main effect has been to make the play darker. For example, "I still believe, in spite of everything, that people are really good at heart" is no longer its ultimate message. Now the line is heard in voiceover as the group is being seized onstage, but it has been restored to its context—an extremely bleak one—in the diary. Kesselman has also deepened the play's Jewish content. Thus, just before their arrest, Anne reproaches Peter for rejecting his heritage: "I'd never turn back on who I am. . . . Don't you realize, Peter, you'll always be Jewish . . . in your soul." In an episode similarly aimed at intensifying the play's Jewishness, Albert Dussel makes a brief appearance alone onstage in a prayer shawl to perform his devotions. (Elided is the fact that Anne in her diary wryly mocks Dussel's piety.)

Another change affecting the play's tone occurs at the beginning and end. Gone is the framing device, in which Otto Frank finds comfort in reading the diary. Now the play opens with the Franks' arrival in the annex and closes with Otto relating the deaths of Anne and the others to the audience. His shocking description of Anne, gleaned from surviving witnesses—"naked, her head shaved, covered with lice"—offers a bitter, almost exploitative contrast to the rosy final image of her in the Hacketts' script, bathed in a "a soft, reassuring smile . . . with courage to meet whatever lies ahead."

But the whole of Kesselman's revision amounts to far less than the sum of its parts. Despite the changes, this is still the same sentimental play about a luminous, flirtatious, idealistic Anne Frank that made the critics swoon 40 years ago. Ben Brantley, in his *Times* review, dubbed this Anne a Proustian "girl in flower," a "rosebud," an "exquisite fawn," her skin aglow "with the promise of miraculous transformations." In the same language Susan Strasberg, the Broadway Anne of 1955, was hailed as a "flowering . . . youngster . . . pure in heart," with the "shining spirit of a young girl." And as if the established image of Anne as a frolicsome teenage saint were not already so potent, it was sealed definitively by the casting of the sixteen-year-old starlet Natalie Portman in the leading role. Pictures in the Playbill given to theatergoers, using soft-focus close-ups, capitalize on Portman's jarringly precocious, Lolita-like beauty as, lips parted, she gazes soulfully outward.

Actually, Portman onstage fails to convey Anne's budding sexuality, to say nothing of her budding intellect. Skipping and twirling about, parading in too-big red high heels and trying on Mrs. van Daan's mink coat, Portman succeeds only in exacting Anne as she was before going into hiding, the "terrible flirt, coquettish and amusing" (in Anne's own later description of herself). Whereas Anne in her diary often observes that her experiences in hiding have transformed her (she has "grown wise within these walls"), in the second act Portman merely furrows her brow and wears a ragged sweater.

Absent from this portrait is the girl who in the annex studied French, English, geography, biology, and art history; who read Greek mythology, biographies of Galileo, Liszt, Charles V, and a book called *Palestine at the Crossroads*. No less absent is the Anne Frank who, on one occasion in January 1943, recorded in her diary:

> I'm seething with rage, yet I can't show it . . . I'd like to scream, . . .
> "Leave me alone, let me have at least one night when I don't cry myself to sleep with my eyes burning and my head pounding. . . . "
> But . . . I can't let them see . . . the wounds they've inflicted on me.

And absent above all is the Anne Frank whom Miep Gies would later recall coming upon bent over her diary, writing:

I'd seen Anne, like a chameleon, go from mood to mood, but
always with friendliness. . . . But I saw a look on her face at this
moment that I'd never seen before. It was a look of dark concentration, as if she had a throbbing headache.

This look pierced me, and I was speechless. She was suddenly
another person there writing at the table.

These sides of Anne are nowhere to be seen in Portman's portrayal, and are
only glancingly alluded to in the revised text of the play.

It may seem curious that a team in possession of the definitive edition
of the diary, and determined to use it to thwart the putative will of Otto
Frank by presenting the "unexpurgated" Anne, should fail so starkly at the
task. But the truth is that editions of the diary have nothing to do with the
matter; Anne's complexity was every bit as evident in the "expurgate"
edition of 1952 as it is in the full-dress edition of 1955. The failure is
Broadway's alone.

This, indeed, may be as good a place as any to attempt, perhaps futilely,
a measure of retroactive justice to the much-maligned man who brought
Anne Frank to the world's attention. After his death in 1980, Otto Frank's
second wife recalled that upon reading Anne's diary, he "discovered that he
had not really known his daughter . . . [that] he had never known anything
about her innermost thoughts, her high ideals, her belief in God and her
progressive ideas." It is perhaps not surprising that Otto Frank was never
able fully to fathom his murdered daughter; his own statements about her
oversimplified her concerns and her ideals. Nevertheless, in the diary he
edited and allowed to be published, he most assuredly allowed her to speak
for herself.

Now that the diary is a world-historical document, it may be difficult
to remember that it began as a private sheaf of papers that Frank was not
obligated to make public at all, let alone in its raw form. In fact, some editing
was essential if only because Anne had two working drafts. But the
unabridged text, in its entirety, Otto Frank willed to the Netherlands State
Institute for War Documentation, thus providing for the publication that
would follow his death.

In 1989, the Institute brought out a 700-page English-language Critical
Edition that systematically compares Anne's original dairy, her own revised
version, and *The Dairy of a Young Girl* published in 1952. (The edition also
contains rich background material and authenticates the diary against the
claims of Holocaust "revisionists.") The more manageable paperback Definitive Edition of 1995, upon which Kesselman drew for the new play, makes a
complete version of the diary easily available to all, in an improved translation.

Technically speaking, the 1995 edition contains 30 percent more material than the 1952 one. But—here is the odd thing—the only discernible differences between the two are, by and large, differences in translation. Aside from these, the Anne Frank of the new edition is the same intellectually precocious, self-absorbed, sexually curious, Jewishly engaged girl to be found in the edition of 1952.

Of course, Otto Frank did make cuts in the manuscripts he had in his possession. Thus, for example, he removed a few "unflattering passages" about his wife Edith and the others; he did so, he said, "out of respect for the dead." But innumerable bitter complaints about Edith Frank, the van Daan parents, and the persnickety Dussel (with whom Anne had to share a room) were retained. Anne's dissatisfaction with her mother remained a major theme of the 1952 edition, though from her self-reproach about it later in the diary it seems quite likely that she herself, had she lived, might have cut the harshest passages.

Some sexual content was also cut in the early editions—less, however, on Otto Frank's initiative than on that of the diary's first international publishers. Mention of menstruation or female breasts was not permitted by the Dutch publisher, though such material appeared in both the German and English editions, as in this passage absent from the 1955 play but added to Kesselman's new script as if to restore material supposedly "suppressed" by Otto Frank:

> Sometimes, when I lie in bed at night, I have a terrible desire to feel my breasts and to listen to the quiet rhythmic beat of my heart . . . I remember that once when I slept with a girlfriend I had a strong desire to kiss her, and that I did do so . . . I asked her whether . . . we should feel one another's breasts, but she refused.

When Anne fell passionately in love with the young Peter van Daan in early 1944, her sexual inquisitiveness increased. Much of their courtship consisted of bashful questions concerning the facts of life. While the 1952 edition did remove explicit references to genitals, contraceptives, virginity, castration, and the like, it is left quite obvious what sorts of things the two adolescents were discussing in their long talks together. More to the point, Anne's introspective account of the actual romance, which appears in all its turbulence in the 1952 edition, is in sharp contrast to the saccharine relationship we are offered in both versions of the play.

If Anne's sexual feelings were on display in 1952, what about her Jewish feelings? Ralph Melnick charges that in editing the diary, Otto Frank "carefully molded . . . an Anne reflective of his own background—secular, uneducated in

Judaism, and anti-Zionist." Like Meyer Levin before him, he accuses Frank of retroactively squelching not only Anne's evolving religiosity and concern with Jewish matters but even her awareness of the degree to which European Jews were imperiled. These accusations have been echoed by Cynthia Ozick, who in the *New Yorker* last October cited Melnick's examples and referred bitterly to Otto's "deracinated temperament."

Otto Frank can indeed be faulted for allowing the German translator of the diary to temper Anne's anti-German sentiments; his excuse was that Anne "by no means measured all Germans by the same yardstick." But it cannot be said that Frank censored those sentiments altogether, since they appeared in full in the English and other editions. One example among many:

> Nice people, the Germans! To think that I was once one of them too! No, Hitler took away our nationality long ago. In fact, Germans and Jews are the greatest enemies in the world.

The German question aside, the charge that Otto Frank distorted the religious and Jewish content of the diary is simply false. Melnick cites brief references to Jewish holidays and to God that were deleted in the 1952 version, but he ignores long passages of equal or much greater import that were left intact, including a mention of Otto's and Anne's nightly ritual of praying together. An examination of the 1989 comparative edition suggests, indeed, that the cuts were made purely for reasons of narrative continuity and not out of animus toward Judaism. The most damning of the supposed omissions adduced by Melnick, about other "Jews who are not in hiding," in fact appears in the entry for May 1, 1943.

Similarly, while Otto Frank could not or would not see that Anne's Jewish consciousness was more assertive than his own, it is untrue that he suppressed it in the diary. The first edition is imbued not only with that consciousness but also with her angry, anguished knowledge of Jewish perse-cution. This passage was written in October 1942:

> Our many Jewish friends are being taken away by the dozen . . . If it is as bad as this in Holland, whatever will it be like in the distant and barbarous regions they are sent to? We assume that most of them are murdered. The English radio speaks of their being gassed.

Most unforgettable is a recurring dream Anne had in 1943 and 1944, in which she envisions a deported Jewish girlfriend, "clothed in rags," "a symbol . . . of the sufferings of . . . all Jews. When I pray for her, I pray for all Jews." Although this friend, Hannah Goslar, who later saw Anne in Bergen-Belsen, was in fact fated to survive the war, Anne is tormented by guilt over her fate "Why should I be chosen to live and she probably to die?"

What is more, the 1952 edition makes it crystal clear that Anne's belief in people being "truly good at heart" was the sentiment not of a naïve idealist but of one who, amid teeming violence and uncertainty, held on to this "cherished hope"—and that is all it was—literally for dear life. Prizing her ideals, Anne also recognized the irony of "rattling on" about them in her desperate circumstances. Her emotions careering between terror and hope, she sought comfort in Jewish faith and Jewish identity:

> If we bear all this suffering and if there are still Jews left, when it is over, then Jews, instead of being doomed, will be held up as an example. Who knows, it might even be our religion from which the world and all peoples learn good . . . God has never deserted our people.

But one must also be careful. Although Anne was unambivalently loyal to the Jews, her own personal aspirations were not centrally bound up with the issue of Jewish identity. She was, among other things, a young patriot of her adopted country ("My first wish after the war is to become a Dutch citizen. I love the Dutch, I love this country, I love the language"). And whereas her sister hoped to "nurse newborns in Palestine," at fourteen and fifteen Anne craved sophistication and glamour. She wanted to study art history in Paris, and yearned to grow into self-reliant womanhood: "If only I can be myself, I'll be satisfied . . . if God lets me live . . . I'll make my voice heard."

Finally, it cannot be stressed enough that Anne's "greatest wish," her burning ambition, was to be a "famous writer." She was right to think that her copious talents ran in this direction. Considered simply as a piece of writing, her diary is extraordinary, depicting with precision and lucidity the highest and lowest moments of a life in hiding, and creating indelible portraits of the seven people who shared it with her. A ten-page account of a theft that almost led to the group's discovery in April 1944 is masterful in its pacing and characterization, as are many other passages. The conversations she records are vivid and spontaneous.

Anne's small collection of other writings, published as *Tales from the Secret Annex*, is more childlike than the diary, but some of her stories—they include nature fables, autobiographical allegories, reminiscences of school pranks, teachers, friendships, and of the time "when we still were part of ordinary, everyday life"—have an almost modernist sparseness that contrasts refreshingly with the density of the diary. There can be little question that, had she lived, this talented, self-conscious, and fiercely ambitious girl would have set out to make her way in the world as a writer, there to succeed or to fail.

Anne Frank saw her personality as a "bundle of contradictions." The phrase is trite, but faithful—more faithful than any of the trite uses to which that personality has been put over the decades at the hands of playwrights and propagandists of one type or another. Her diary has been represented as the quintessential coming-of-age story, a tale of first love and moist adolescent idealism; as epitomizing (in the words of George Stevens, who directed the 1959 film) the "triumph of the human spirit" over evil; or, in today's less optimistic but no less falsifying terms, as symbolizing the betrayed hopes and courage, the destroyed humanity, of six million victims. Outraged by the real and alleged distortions perpetrated on Anne's spirit, Cynthia Ozick has gone so far as to suggest that it would be better had her diary simply "burned, vanished."

It was, however, precisely against the sure prospect of oblivion that in August 1944 Miep Gies went up to the secret annex on the heels of the SS and hid the document, intact and unburned. There is no need to rely on Broadway, or any intermediary, for a true sense of the brilliant bundle of contradictions that was Anne Frank. Anyone who has a mind to can still turn to the work that Miep Gies rescued and that Otto Frank, despite misgivings, and to his everlasting credit, brought into the light of day. In its pages, in whatever edition, his daughter has always spoken for herself.

BARBARA CHIARELLO

The Utopian Space of a Nightmare: The Diary of Anne Frank

Defining a Holocaust text as utopian literature verges on the impossible. How can works depicting imaginary better worlds emerge from people forced to live in a Nazi-created Hell? How could Jews—the prime objectives of Hitler's Final Solution—contemplate the ideal? How could a person depict good, too-good-to-be-true, while coping with evil, too-evil-to-comprehend? Yet detailing a utopia while being threatened by an ever-encroaching dystopia may mean spiritual survival to a victim of the Holocaust's fury.

Circumstances forced Anne Frank to reject More's historical definition of utopia as a place too good to be true. In *Socialism: The Active Utopia*, Zygmunt Bauman acknowledged the importance of circumstances when he wrote " . . . utopian ideals . . . are shaped . . . under the double pressure of the galvanising feeling of deprivation and the chastening squeeze of omnipresent and stubborn realities." Anne had to create a utopia—"the expression of the desire for a better way of being and living"—or perish in despair. Other Holocaust victims chose despair. Charlotte Salomon, a Jewish painter born in Berlin, fled to France in 1939 at the age of 22. One of her works was captioned, "I cannot bear this life, I cannot bear these times." But when Nazism pushed 13-year-old Anne out of her customary world into a new one, she used her diary to both depict an imaginary better place and to prove the possibility of positive changes in the present. Anne acknowledges

From *Utopian Studies* 5:1 (1994). © 1994 by the Society for Utopian Studies.

the compensatory utopian intention of her diary in her first sentence, which precedes the first officially dated entry, "I hope you will be a great support and comfort to me."

Evaluating *The Diary of Anne Frank* for inclusion in utopian literature would be easier if the academic community clearly defined utopia. But "working definitions range from the refusal of any definition at all," Levitas writes, "through definitions in terms of form, form and content, function, function and form." As she argues for a broad definition, she unintentionally seems to welcome Anne's diary to the field.

The "emphasis has changed from the presentation of finished perfection to a more open exploration in which the construction of the individual, and thus the question of another way of being, has become the central issue." *The Diary of Anne Frank* is clearly a "construction of the individual" that addresses "the question of another way of being."

Another obstacle this work must overcome to be accepted as utopian literature also serves as its unique strength: the diary form. Custom often limits utopian expression to book-length fiction, but the form Anne chose gave her work the authority, credibility, immediacy and a straight-forward, non-didactic tone unique to this genre. Anne could have expressed her message of hope in various other forms—indeed, she did write several essays and short stories while in hiding that were first published in part under the title *Tales From the House Behind.* But the diary form also fulfills another of Levitas' assertions: "the pursuit of a better way of being . . . may mean the pursuance of spiritual or psychological states."

Anne began writing a second version of her diary in May 1944, with the hope of publishing "a book entitled *Het Achterhuis* after the war. Whether I shall succeed or not, I cannot say, but my diary will be a great help." If she had lived to accomplish this goal, she might hve chosen another way to express her thoughts. Yet having her words in dairy form also bypasses several traditional artifices, such as reliance on reference, sacred writings, and contrived characters and dialogues that many utopian texts use to establish authority. Other utopian works, like Ernest Callenbach's *Ectopia* (1975), Eugene Zamiatin's *We* (1924), and George Orwell's *Nineteen Eighty-Four* (1949), include this form to add credibility and immediacy. But Anne's diary is more believable than fictional uses of the form. Even though her work, like all diaries, is a highly selective portrayal of reality—it contains only that part of the "truth" the writer perceives and selects for inclusion—the form speaks with the compelling voice of someone who has lived its message. It is a voice that, to many readers, will ring more convincingly than the voices of imaginary visitors to imaginary worlds. True, a diarist can come close to, but never succeed, at duplicating the "experience." But Anne's honest tone helps to overcome this problem. She acknowledged: "Although I tell you a lot, still, even so, you only know very little of our lives." Furthermore, at least the first version of this diary—unlike Benjamin Franklin's or even Frederick Douglass's—seems more truthful because Anne wrote it for herself, not with the expectation it would be published and widely read.

Anne's religion and youth add credibility to the diary form. Since Anne was Jewish, this work is even more compelling as a firsthand account of a person who lived through the events, not as an outside observer, but as a victim. As a thirteen to fifteen year old, she's too naïve to be subtly manipulative, or at least the reader is less likely to assume manipulative intent. Anne writes with an innocence that allows the reader to identify with her. She hasn't yet learned to hide behind barriers; she's less afraid of exposing herself than many adults who have learned to censor their innermost thoughts, especially writers concerned with earning financial support from their audience. Her age also supports Ernst Bloch's theory of the Not-Yet-Conscious where he believed the universal utopian impulse resides and which is at its best in "youth, times which are on the point of changing, creative expression. . . . With puberty begins the mystery of women, the mystery of life, the mystery of knowledge. . . . If youth occurs in revolutionary times . . . then it really does know what forward dreaming is all about." Bloch also argues that utopia is more than forward dreaming, "not taken only as emotion, . . . but more essentially as a directing act of a cognitive kind." Indeed, Anne's diary not only lists her experiences, it offers a blueprint on how to live. When Pfeffer arrived on November 17, 1942, she presented him with typed "Secret Annexe Rules" which included, "Use of language: Speak softly at all times, by order! All civilized languages are permitted, therefore no German!" Anne's humor—part of her coping arsenal—takes the sting (and boredom) out of the didactic nature inherent in many utopian works.

The diary reinforces her communication style. Anne doesn't preach; she illustrates. She creates a short story per entry. She presents vital images that ignite feelings and thoughts, creating blanks or "gaps," to use Wolfgang Iser's term, for the reader to fill. The diary form parallels her intent. Each "yours truly" gives the reader a pause to acknowledge feelings and formulate conclusions on each entry before proceeding to the next salutation. "Yours truly, Anne" forms a natural break, like ending a letter. Then "Dear Kitty" invites the reader back into the next communication. This stopping and starting also functions to mark time. Although Anne didn't realize this, the date at the top of each entry mimics the tick-tock of the time bomb the reader knows will ultimately explode her utopia. The date also underlines her subtle exhortation to live each day with joy and hope.

The diary form also adds even more immediacy than a straightforward first-person account in fiction or autobiography. As Kenneth M. Roemer asserts in his introduction to *America as Utopia*, "A literary utopia is . . . a 'fiction' that encourages readers to experience vicariously a culture that represents a prescriptive, normative alternative to their own culture." Anne pulls the reader into her culture each time she begins an entry for a vicarious experience that ends when she signs off in a manner that establishes her immediate presence. The "I" in a fictional narrative can too often blend into a third-person blur. In such a text, the reader may forget just who the narrator is and get lost in the events, descriptions, or other characters. Not here. Anne even signs her name differently—mostly it's a simple Anne, some-times it's Anne Mary, Anne M. Frank or Anne Mary Frank—thus reminding the reader, "This is me on this particular day." Given the overwhelming number of Holocaust victims, this constant repetition prevents the reader from viewing the number in a detached, alienated manner, from becoming numbed and overwhelmed by incomprehensibility. The reader must experi-ence the horror of seeing Anne and, by implication, millions like her as suffering individuals.

Anne lives in her words. On April 4, 1944, she eerily acknowledged this possibility: "I want to go on living even after my death! And therefore I am grateful to God for giving me this gift, this possibility . . . of writing, of expressing all that is in me." The diary allows her to express this wish directly to readers who may shake their heads in utopian joy, glad she realized they would share in her immortality. Since the form makes it impossible for Anne to write about her own death, the text cannot refute this pretense.

When Anne and her family began another way of life, survival meant retreat. Faced with annihilation, the Franks entered a small space they would share with three, then four others. Instead of entering a bigger and better world, these eight hoped to survive by shrinking into almost nothing-ness. Their utopia wasn't a vast, expansive, visible model. Being seen by the Gestapo meant death. While typical late nineteenth- and early twentieth-century Utopian works, like Edward Bellamy's *Looking Backward* (1888) and Charolotte Perkins Gilman's *Herland* (1919) followed the prevailing assump-tion by presenting their ideal world on a society—or country-wide state, *The Diary of Anne Frank* used another approach to create the genre's requisite feeling of freedom. In doing so, this work may have pioneered a contempo-rary utopian approach to space. Anne Frank's work challenges George Orwell's *Nineteen Eight-Four,* where dystopia equals confinement to Room 101 and foreshadows smaller-scale modern utopias such as Marge Piercy's Mattapoisett in *Woman on the Edge of Time* (1976) and Ursula K. Le Guin's "Sur" (1982) and the worlds discussed by Robert Plank in his essay "The

Modern Shrunken Utopia." Like Burris in *Walden Two* and the protagonists in many feminist utopias, Anne finds the ideal in small communities, interpersonal relationships, and inner growth. Again Levitas seems to be referring to Anne's diary when she writes, "contemporary utopias . . . tend to withdraw into the interstices of a seemingly irredeemable actually existing society rather than confidently heralding its transformation." Anne does this on two levels: she withdraws from Nazi-occupied Europe and then from the petty politics of family and strangers living in confined quarters into the utopian womb of her diary.

Since Anne Frank refused to retreat into a utopian fantasy more in keeping with More's good—but no—place, her work can be seen as a fitting illustrative companion text to several modern theorists besides Levitas. Forced into a real space, she made it good; thus supplying hope to post-Holocaust scholars like Marie Louise Berneri who could no longer assume civilization's steady march toward progress. Since the diary deals with Nazism—a seemingly universal evil—it serves as the battleground for an ongoing question in the field of utopian studies: "Is the good society more than a matter of personal preference?" *The Diary of Anne Frank* straddles both sides of other current quandaries: it is at once itself and its opposite. The work is both imaginary and historical—a distinction Berneri struggles with as she tries to define utopia; the theoretical and the practical; the status quo and the alternative, and the idea and the change. The text is utopian in form and function—not only does the diary adhere to many utopian conventions, but it sets out a blueprint for how to create a utopian inner space instead of focusing on implementing the good society. Levitas's new definition of utopia supports this interpretation: "we learn a lot about the experience of living under any set of conditions by reflecting upon the desires which those conditions generate and yet leave unfulfilled. For that is the space which utopia occupies."

This innovative way of redefining utopian space was not a literary exercise for Anne Frank. Forced into confinement to avoid unimaginable suffering and to escape the kind of existing society utopian socialists like Saint-Simon, Fourier and Owen would describe as "unjust, immoral and generally insupportable"—she could have retreated to madness or suicide. She did neither. Instead, she chose to enter a utopia that isn't an insane denial of reality, but the space between what is and what one hopes, a here and now made more tolerable by detailing what can be, a society "characterised by cooperation rather than antagonism" as the utopian socialists envisioned. Through her diary, she reinterprets her present and constructs a survival manual for overcoming a world gone mad—what Bauman called relativising the present: " . . . by scanning the field of the possible in which the real occupies merely a tiny plot, utopias pave the way for a critical attitude and a critical activity which alone can transform the present predicament of man." Utilizing many conventions of traditional utopian fictions, Anne Frank's diary details the imaginary world she created that pushed horrific reality into a tiny, and therefore, manageable plot.

Several of the utopian conventions that were particularly crucial to her imagined better world include: a journey to an alternative place, a prevailing attitude more hopeful than the reader's, a visitor and a guide who engage in a dialogue, a conversion narrative, a message the visitor returns with, foils, and an assured tone proclaiming that the alternate world is definitely superior to the reader's world. Gradually, as one gets into an effective utopian text, the reader escapes from a cruel, imperfect reality into a kinder, and more just, society. Anne Frank's work fulfills these criteria.

II

The openings of many well-known utopian texts, like *Utopia*, *Looking Backward*, *Herland* and *Walden Two*, are ground in familiar realities. Similarly, this diary begins during the least fearful and most comfortable time for both the writer and the post-Holocaust reader. Anne's first entries tell of her 13th birthday celebrations at home and at school before she goes into hiding. She writes about starting to date, and, perhaps, falling in love with, a young man she has recently met. All this chatty, normal teenager talk ends on July 8, 1942 when she says, "years seem to have passed between Sunday and now . . . it is as if the whole world had turned upside down."

Anne's journey may seem mundane compared to the time travel and strange voyages of other utopian travelers. Her family left their home to live in rooms located on the second floor, third floor, and attic of a warehouse owned by her father. But the journey Anne takes is spiritual as well as physical. She uses a common utopian device, traveling forward in time to a new world, to explain her feelings in the above excerpt. Her dated entries show that the Sunday she feels was years ago was really only three days before, but Anne has leapt into a utopia that she must believe promises life.

Further entries illustrate how sharply Anne differentiates between the utopia she has created and the nightmare surrounding it. Anne speaks of her "beautiful bathroom" and writes "although it sounds mad, I think it is the best place of all"; her "secret den," of events in "our little passage" and "our superpractical exquisite little 'Secret Annexe.'" Anne's language transforms these rooms into another world parallel to the real world outside. She speaks of "sitting cozily in the main office" and asserts, it is "quiet and safe here."

She becomes uncomfortable leaving, even to go to a Christmas celebration in one of the warehouse offices. " . . . (it made me shudder and wish I was safely upstairs again). . . . "

Anne takes a journey when she goes "upstairs again," a journey signifying more than simply ascending an ordinary flight of steps.

> I see the 8 of us with our "Secret Annexe" as if we were a little piece of blue heaven, surrounded by black, black rain clouds. The round, clearly defined spot where we stand is still safe but the clouds gather more and more closely about us. . . . We all look down below where people are fighting each other, we look above, where it is quiet and beautiful, and meanwhile we are cut off by the great dark mass, . . . which stands before us as an impenetrable wall: it tries to crush us but cannot do so yet.

She has turned the secret annex into her unreachable, sane, and happy nest, even though it's actually quite small, hot in the summer, smelly when circumstances force the inhabitants to use huge glass jars as chamber pots, and ultimately no safer for Anne than the reality she's left. Although Anne's "het achterhuis," like any imaginary heaven, cannot save her, her utopian attitude prevents "the great dark mass" from crushing her by keeping her spirit alive.

Of course, not all incidences of hiding away in confined areas constitute creating utopian spaces. American slave Harriet A. Jacobs hid for several years, not for survival, but to keep her children from being sold as plantation slaves. Her much smaller hiding space—nine feet long, seven feet wide and three feet at the highest—may explain Jacobs's more negative attitude, but it is this martyred stance that prevents *Incidents in the Life of a Slave Girl* (1861) from being considered utopian. Told through the words of Linda Brent, the narrator she created, Jacobs wrote: "Dark thoughts passed through my mind as I lay there day after day. I tried to be thankful for my little cell, dismal as it was, and even to love it, as part of the price I had to pay for the redemption of my children."

Hawthorne wrote in his allegory, "The Hall of Fantasy," that " . . . even the actual becomes ideal . . . in hope." Anne armors herself with hope to carry her through irritating, everyday problems, on-going anti-German war events that fail to free her, and near discovery. Hope tells her not to question her ultimate survival and to prepare actively to re-enter post-Nazi Holland. While other utopian texts imaginatively solve the problems of poverty, overwork, or crime, this work shows how hope can (at least emotionally) detoxify a poisonous time and function "not merely as fictitious compensation for the discomforts of experienced reality, but a venturing beyond that reality."

> When the Frank family arrived at 263 Prisengracht, the living
> room and all the other rooms were chock full of rubbish, inde-
> scribably so. . . . We had to start clearing up immediately if we
> wished to sleep on decent beds that night. Mummy and Margot
> were not in a fit state to take part; they were tired and lay down on
> their unmade beds, they were wretched . . . but the two "clearers-
> up" of the family Daddy and myself, wanted to start at once. . . .
>   We hadn't had a bit of anything warm the whole day but we
> didn't care, Mummy and Margot were too tired and keyed up to
> eat and Daddy and I were to busy.

Anne is not one to be wretched over indescribably messed up rooms, or an indescribably messed up world. Interestingly, she uses the Dutch word "opruimers," which has been translated into "clearers-up" instead of cleaners-up, to describe herself and her father as if recognizing her role as more of a remover of chaos than of dust and dirt.

Since Anne recognizes the gloom, her utopia isn't rooted in denial. On November 19, 1942, she wrote: "In the evenings when it's dark, I often see rows of good, innocent people accompanied by crying children . . . bullied and knocked about until they almost drop. Nobody is spared, old people, children, babies, expectant mothers, the sick each and all join in the march of death." Then the next day, she writes, "The news about the Jews had not really penetrated through to us until now." Friedrich Pfeffer, who had just been invited to share their hiding place, gave them the latest information about the Jewish friends and acquaintances they had left behind.

Anne consciously chooses to triumph over the horror. "It won't do us any good or help those on the outside to go on being as gloomy as we are at the moment. . . . Must I keep thinking about those people whatever I am doing? Ought I then to cry the whole day long? No, that I can't do."

So Anne laughs. She laughs at her everyday discomforts: "We have a moth biscuit with syrup [the biscuit tin is kept in the wardrobe which is full of mothballs] and have fun."

> One afternoon we couldn't go to the lavatory because there were
> visitors in the office; however, Peter had to pay an urgent call. So
> he didn't pull the plug. He put a notice up on the lavatory door
> to warn us, with "S.V.P. gas" on it. Of course he meant to put
> "Beware of gas"; but he thought the other looked more genteel.
> He hadn't got the faintest notion it meant "if you please."

She laughs at her ineptitude: "I must cut Daddy's hair. Pim [her pet name for her father] maintains that he will never have another barber after the war, as I do the job so well. If only I didn't snip his ear so often!" And after one of their cats used some wood shavings in the attic as a litter box and its urine dripped down into their barrel of potatoes: "The ceiling was dripping. . . . I was doubled up with laughter, it really was such a scream."

Within the humor, Anne has shown us that her world isn't perfect, again heralding modern utopias that theorist Tom Moylan suggests "focus on the continuing presence of difference and imperfection within utopian society itself." Anne's utopia is in keeping with Lyman Tower Sargent's point in his introduction to *British and American Utopian Literature, 1516–1985*: "It is important to realize that most utopias are not projected as perfect worlds but as much better ones."

Anne not only used humor in her diary to coat the real unpleasantness of hiding, she searched for and exaggerated the glimmers of hope in the war news of her day. She responds to Churchill's famous lines with overflowing joy, ignoring his equivocation. "This is not the end," Churchill said. "It is not even the beginning of the end. But it is perhaps the end of the beginning." After quoting these words in her diary, she writes, "Do you see the difference? There is certainly reason for optimism."

On July 21, 1944, instead of bemoaning the failed attempted assassination of Hitler, she writes: " . . . now things are going well at last. Yes, really, they are going well! Super news! An attempt has been made on Hitler's life and not even by Jewish communists or English capitalists this time, but by a proud German general, and what's more, he's a count, and still quite young." Had Hitler been killed, Anne and her family might have survived. But Anne never contemplates how this failed assassination may result in her death or, at the very least, a longer time in hiding. Instead, she frames the event in an even more positive light as she continues in the same entry, "Perhaps the Divine Power tarried on purpose in getting him out of the way, because it would be much easier and more advantageous to the Allies if the impeccable Germans kill each other off."

This approach parallels the approach of her co-religionist Karl Mannheim, who was exiled to England by the Nazis in 1933, when he stated, "Utopias [as opposed to ideologies] . . . succeed through counteractivity in transforming the existing historical reality into one more in accord with their own conceptions." Her work also exemplifies that of Bloch, a radical German-Jewish intellectual who was also exiled in the thirties, when he called for daydreams "not in the sense of merely contemplative reason which takes things as they are and as they stand, but of participating reason which takes them as they go, and also as they could go better." While Anne Frank was not aware of Mannheim and Bloch's more global approaches to change, she nevertheless framed her world within their philosophies. One explanation for their common attitudes may be Judaism's emphasis on the here and now, as opposed to the utopian Christian heaven.

Jacobs illustrates this other worldly focus and resigned approach in the following excerpt:

> Sometimes I thought God was a compassionate Father, who would forgive my sins for the sake of my sufferings. At other times, it seemed to me that there was no justice or mercy in the divine garment. I asked why the curse of slavery was permitted to exist, and why I had been so persecuted and wronged from youth upward. These things took the shape of mystery, which is to this day not so clear to my soul as I trust it will be hereafter.

Unlike Jacobs, Anne remains rooted in her utopian present even when faced with near discovery. Although the inhabitants of the "secret annexe" are careful to be quiet when they know workers are about, they are afraid they were overheard and reported by burglars who had entered the warehouse the previous night. Anne writes "I prepared myself for the return of the police, then we'd have to say that we were in hiding; they would either be good Dutch people [the police], then we'd be saved, or N.S.B.ers [The Dutch National Socialist Movement], then we'd have to bribe them!" Of course, this isn't what ultimately happens when they are discovered, but until then the utopian prism Anne holds up as she views real events keeps her from spiritual death.

On Friday, August 4, 1944, the outside world broke this prism. Harry Paape, under the auspices of the Netherlands State Institute for War Documentation, obtained oral and written accounts from those eyewitnesses that survived for his report on what happened that day. The following is a synopsis of his findings: When a German officer and several Dutch men in civilian clothes entered the warehouse, they were directed upstairs by a worker named Van Maaren, believed by some to be the informer. These men approached the bookcase that hid the entrance to the "secret annexe" with their guns drawn and demanded it be opened, obviously knowing what they would find. According to Otto Frank, Anne's father, the Dutch officials appeared to belong to the German Sicherheitdienst (Security Service, or SD). While waiting for a truck that would transport the inhabitants to headquarters of the Amsterdam Bureau of the Commander of the Security Police and Security Service, the German, Karl Silberbauer, discovered Mr. Frank had been a German Reserve lieutenant during World War I.

"At once, Silberbauer's attitude changed," Frank told the Dutch detective tht examined him after the war, "he even looked for a moment as if he was going to snap to attention in front of me." Later, Silberbauer seemed ready to accept a bribe from a Dutch friend that had brought food and supplies to the "secrete annexe." But this strategy, that Anne had hoped would save them, proved futile. "I'm sorry but I can't do anything for you," Silberbauer told Miep Gies, "I'm not senior enough."

Anne created a utopian space where she could hope; a place where she saw herself alive after the war. As Levitas explains, "utopia is the expression of desire and desire may outstrip hope while not necessarily outstripping possibility," but in this case, Anne's desire may have outstripped possibility and not hope. Except for the very rare moments of introspection, Anne lives for the future she assumes will be hers. She maintains that the curtains she and her father put up the first day they arrived are "not to come down until we emerge from here." She has decided to work hard at her studies, including French where she plans to "manage to pump in five irregular verbs per day," because she "doesn't want to be in the first form" when she's fourteen or fifteen. Later, she says, "We often discuss postwar problems, for example, how one ought to address servants." Several of her concerns and desires center on "after the war." "I'm afraid I shall use up all my brains too quickly, and I haven't got so very many. Then I shall not have any left for when the war is over." "I can hardly wait for the day that I shall be able to comb through the public library." When she and Peter get close, she doesn't worry if they will survive, instead she wonders how their relationship will progress: " . . . I don't know what he will be like when he grows up, nor do I know whether we should love each other enough to marry."

By assuming a better future—which in her case, is any future at all—Anne delineates a vast utopian space where she can look past the present, inspiring those who are faced with horrible circumstances beyond their control to do the same. Her attitude enlarges two cramped spaces: the physically small "Secret Annexe," and a depression-generated emotional cocoon that she refuses to enter. In conventional utopian terminology, she takes on the role of a guide. The visitor is Kitty; an imaginary audience she created to address in her diary. Anne makes Kitty her companion in retreat from the madness: "I don't want to set down a series of bald facts . . . I want this diary to be my friend, and I shall call my friend Kitty." She welcomes Kitty into her utopia with playful reassurance, telling her "it's more like being on vacation in a very peculiar boardinghouse."

Anne continues to sugarcoat reality for Kitty by showing her how imagination can be a powerful coping mechanism. "When I get up in the morning, which is . . . a very unpleasant process, I jump out of bed thinking to myself: 'You'll be back in a second.'" "If I have to eat something that I simply can't stand; I put my plate in front of me, pretend that it is something delicious, look at it as little as possible, and before I know where I am, it is gone."

When the terror outside spills into Anne's world, she shields Kitty. On February 3, 1944, she reported overhearing a conversation among the adults that ended with the following: " . . . it's a fact that in Poland and Russia millions and millions of people have been murdered and gassed." Instead of pondering these facts, she reassures Kitty; and herself: "Kitty, I'll leave it at that, spare you further details. I myself keep very quiet and don't take any notice of the fuss and excitement." After burglars have broken into the warehouse, the inhabitants of the "secret annexe" assume neighbors will call the police to investigate. When the police arrive, Anne hears them climbing up the stairs to their hiding place, rattling the swinging cupboard that disguises the entrance to "het achterhuis." Anne feared immediate capture: she wrote "this moment is indescribable."

Contrasting Anne's approach with Jacobs's further elucidates the utopian intention of Anne's diary as opposed to Jacobs's purpose in writing her after-the-fact narrative in diary form. "I have not exaggerated the wrongs inflicted by Slavery" Jacobs wrote in her preface, "on the contrary, my descriptions fall far short of the facts. . . . I have not written my experiences . . . to excite sympathy for my sufferings. But I do earnestly desire to arouse the women of the North to a realizing sense of the condition of two millions of women in the South, still in bondage, suffering what I suffered, and most of them far worse."

Unlike Jacobs, and other inhabitants of the "secret annexe" who function as foils, Anne's purpose prevents her from dwelling on the worst. Her utopia functions the way Bloch describes a concrete utopia as "more centrally turned towards the world: of overtaking the natural course of events." She sees the present and consciously alters it in her entries, thus supporting Raymond William's contention that "what makes something utopian is not just a quality of otherness, but the element of transformation, requiring continuity and connectedness to the present. And the transformation . . . is a willed transformation, not one which comes about by technological change or the alteration of external circumstances." Anne couldn't affect her external circumstances, but by writing down her perceptions she willed the transformation of the Nazi-induced present into her own utopian space. Early on, she used her mother and sister to show Kitty what not to do, contrasting their collapsing with Anne's clearing up when the Frank family first went into hiding. In the following excerpt, she compares her mother's approach to melancholy with hers.

Mummy['s] . . . counsel when one feels melancholy is: "Think of all the misery in the world and be thankful that you are not sharing in it." My advice is: " . . . think of all the beauty that's still left in and around you and be happy!"

I don't see how Mummy's idea can be right, because then how are you supposed to behave if you go through the misery yourself? Then you are lost. On the contrary, I've found that there is always some beauty left, if only you look for it. . . .

Anne says focus on the beauty to escape the misery. She concludes: "He who has courage and faith will never perish in misery!"

Her thoughts went beyond facts to manufacture a resiliency to depression and defeat. The diary itself thus takes on another characteristic of a traditional utopia, the conversion narrative. Anne's conversion culminates with a poignant declaration of her firm faith in ideals "in spite of everything"—the overriding message for her audience of post-Holocaust readers. She sees how despondency destroys the soul and counterattacks it with a credo she sets down in the third from final entry in her diary, two-and-a-half weeks before the Gestapo was led to "het achterhuis."

"That's the difficulty in these times," Anne wrote on Saturday, July 15, 1944 after about two years and two weeks in hiding.

Ideals, dreams and cherished hopes rise within us, only to meet the horrible truth and be shattered. It's really a wonder that I haven't dropped all my ideals, because they seem so absurd and impossible to carry out. Yet I keep them, because in spite of everything I still believe that people are really good at heart.

I simply can't build up my hopes on a foundation consisting of confusion, misery, and death, I see the world gradually being turned into a wilderness, I hear the ever approaching thunder, which will destroy us too, I can feel the sufferings of millions and yet, if I look into the heavens, I think that it will all come right, that this cruelty too will end, and that peace and tranquility will return again. In the meantime, I must uphold my ideals, for perhaps the time will come when I shall be able to carry them out!

III

Directly and succinctly, Anne explained why she delineated an imaginary better world when reality dictated otherwise, thus addressing Levitas's assertion that "sometimes utopia embodies more than an image of what the good life would be and becomes a claim about what it could and should be: the wish that things might be otherwise becomes a conviction that it does not have to be like this." Anne's insistence on changing the present—if only in her diary—again underscores a perspective shared by other Jewish writers like Mannheim who wrote, "men, while thinking, are also acting." By filtering the present through her words, Anne performs as one of Paul Tillich's "bearers of utopia . . . those who are able to transform reality" and delineates a utopia that does "transform reality in its own image." Anne's diary thus addresses a concern Levitas has with Mannheim. Levitas states "to identify an idea as a utopia . . . we have to establish that the idea was instrumental in effecting the change, which in practice is very difficult to do even with the benefit of hindsight." As pointed out in the introduction, Anne's work is both the idea and the change. As many of the above examples illustrate, it is precisely her ideas that changed her world.

Anne not only could, but had to write utopian literature as an affirmation of her "ideals, dreams, and cherished hopes." She had to fill the space opened up by Bloch—"the risen horizon that is rising even higher"—or as Levitas elucidates Bloch's Not-Yet-Become—"the space that . . . requires utopia in order that humanity may be able to imagine, will and effect the future." As Tillich expressed it, "all utopias strive to negate the negative itself in human existence; it is the negative in existence which makes the idea of utopia necessary." *The Diary of Anne Frank* blares a message of hope and direction amid the Holocaust-induced pessimistic view of humanity and as a tribute to the utopian force within the soul of a single human being. Anne exemplifies Bloch's positive conclusion to this first volume of *The Principle of Hope*: "Mankind and the world carry enough good future; no plan is itself good without this fundamental belief within it."

IV

Perhaps there are over 15 million copies of Anne Frank's diary, a well-attended museum at the former "het achterhuis," and a recently published Dutch-language children's book (*Anne Frank* about her life before the Holocaust, because Anne offers more than Elie Wiesel's view of a Holocaust utopia: "In war years, another piece of bread is Utopia." Wiesel wrote this after spending years in concentration camps while Anne Frank wrote her diary before she was sent to one. This may or may not explain why Anne can concentrate more on feeding and expanding the soul, not the body; the reader's soul as well as her own. Instead of assuming the impossibility of writing utopian literature during a time when a great deal of political, technological, scientific, and religious energy sought to empower evil, one could assume the opposite: such repression of good demands unrealistic hope and unreasonable courage. As her father, Otto Frank, wrote the introduction to *A Tribute to Anne Frank*, "However touching and sincere the expressions of sympathy I receive may be, I always reply that it is not enough to think of Anne with pity or admiration. Her diary should be a source of inspiration toward the realization of the ideals and hopes she expressed in it." In the midst of horror, Anne Frank certainly made a utopian assumption by writing a survival manual for preserving ideals, thereby providing the hope we sometimes despair of finding. "The dream becomes a vision only when hope is invested in an agency capable of transformation. The political problem remains the search for that agency." *The Diary of Anne Frank* asserts that the agency capable of transformation is one of us at a time.

CYNTHIA OZICK

Who Owns Anne Frank?

If Anne Frank had not perished in the criminal malevolence of Bergen-Belsen early in 1945, she would have marked her sixty-eighth birthday last June. And even if she had not kept the extraordinary diary through which we know her it is likely that we would number her among the famous of this century—though perhaps not so dramatically as we do now. She was born to be a writer. At thirteen, she felt her power; at fifteen, she was in command of it. It is easy to imagine—had she been allowed to live—a long row of novels and essays spilling from her fluent and ripening pen. We can be certain (as certain as one can be of anything hypothetical) that her mature prose would today be noted for its wit and acuity, and almost as certain that the trajectory of her work would be closer to that of Nadine Gordimer, say, than to that of Françoise Sagan. As an international literary presence, she would be thick rather than thin. "I want to go on living even after my death!" she exclaimed in the spring of 1944.

This was more than an exaggerated adolescent flourish. She had already intuited what greatness in literature might mean, and she clearly sensed the force of what lay under her hand in the pages of her diary: a conscious literary record of frightened lives in daily peril; an explosive document aimed directly at the future. In her last months, she was assiduously polishing phrases and editing passages with an eye to postwar publication.

From *The New Yorker* (October 6, 1997). © 1997 by The New Yorker Magazine, Inc.

Het Achterhuis, as she called her manuscript, in Dutch—"the house behind," often translated as "the secret annex"—was hardly intended to be Anne Frank's last word; it was conceived as the forerunner work of a professional woman of letters.

Yet any projection of Anne Frank as a contemporary figure is an unholy speculation: it tampers with history, with reality, with deadly truth. "When I write," she confided, "I can shake off all my cares. My sorrow disappears, my spirits are revived!" But she could not shake off her capture and annihilation, and there are no diary entries to register and memorialize the snuffing of her spirit. Anne Frank was discovered, seized, and deported; she and her mother and sister and millions of others were extinguished in a program calculated to assure the cruelest and most demonically inventive human degradation. The atrocities she endured were ruthlessly and purposefully devised, from indexing by tattoo through systematic starvation to factory-efficient murder. She was designated to be erased from the living, to leave no grave, no sign, no physical trace of any kind. Her fault—her crime—was having been born a Jew, and as such she was classified among those who had no right to exist: not as a subject people, not as an inferior breed, not even as usable slaves. The military and civilian apparatus of an entire society was organized to obliterate her as a contaminant, in the way of a noxious and repellent insect. Zyklon B, the lethal fumigant poured into the gas chambers, was, pointedly, a roach poison.

Anne Frank escaped gassing. One month before liberation, not yet sixteen, she died of typhus fever, an acute infectious disease carried by lice. The precise date of her death has never been determined. She and her sister, Margot, were among three thousand six hundred and fifty-nine women transported by cattle car from Auschwitz to the merciless conditions of Bergen-Belsen, a barren tract of mud. In a cold, wet autumn, they suffered through nights on flooded straw in overcrowded tents, without light, surrounded by latrine ditches, until a violent hail storm tore away what had passed for shelter. Weakened by brutality, chaos, and hunger, fifty thousand men and women—insufficiently clothed, tormented by lice—succumbed, many to the typhus epidemic.

Anne Frank's final diary entry, written on August 1, 1944, ends introspectively—a meditation on a struggle for moral transcendence set down in a mood of wistful gloom. It speaks of "turning my heart inside out, the bad part on the outside and the good part on the inside," and of "trying to find a way to become what I'd like to be and what I could be if . . . if only there were no other people in the world." Those curiously self-subduing ellipses are the diarist's own; they are more than merely a literary effect—they signify a child's muffled bleat against confinement, the last whimper of a prisoner in a cage. Her circumscribed world had a population of eleven—the three Dutch protectors who came and went, supplying the necessities of life, and the eight in hiding: the van Daans, their son Peter, Albert Dussel, and the four Franks. Five months earlier, on May 26, 1944, she had railed against the stress of living invisibly—a tension never relieved, she asserted, "not once in the two years we've been here. How much longer will this increasingly oppressive, unbearable weight press down on us?" And, several paragraphs on, "What will we do if we're . . . no, I mustn't write that down. But the question won't let itself be pushed to the back of my mind today; on the contrary, all the fear I've ever felt is looming before me in all its horror. . . . I've asked myself again and again whether it wouldn't have been better if we hadn't gone into hiding, if we were dead now and didn't have to go through this misery. . . . Let something happend soon. . . . Nothing can be more crushing than this anxiety. Let the end come, however cruel." And on April 11, 1944: "We are Jews in chains."

The diary is not a genial document, despite its author's often vividly satiric exposure of what she shrewdly saw as "the comical side of life in hiding." Its reputation for uplift is, to say it plainly, nonsensical. Anne Frank's written narrative, moreover, is not the story of Anne Frank, and never has been. That the diary is miraculous, a self-aware work of youthful genius, is not in question. Variety of pace and tone, insightful humor, insupportable suspense, adolescent love pangs and disappointments, sexual curiosity, moments of terror, moments of elation, flights of idealism and prayer and psychological acumen—all these elements of mind and feeling and skill brilliantly enliven its pages. There is, besides, a startlingly precocious comprehension of the progress of the war on all fronts. The survival of the little group in hiding is crucially linked to the timing of the Allied invasion. Overhead the bombers, roaring to their destinations, make the house quake; sometimes the bombs fall terrifyingly close. All in all, the diary is a chronicle of trepidation, turmoil, alarm. Even its report of quieter periods of reading and study express the hush of imprisonment. Meals are boiled lettuce and rotted potatoes; flushing the single toilet is forbidden for ten hours at a time. There is shooting at night. Betrayal and arrest always threaten. Anxiety and immobility rule. It is a story of fear.

But the diary in itself, richly crammed though it is with incident and passion, cannot count as Anne Frank' s story. A story may not be said to be a story if the end is missing. And because the end is missing, the story of Anne Frank in the fifty years since *The Diary of a Young Girl* was first published has been bowdlerized, distorted, transmuted, traduced, reduced; it has been infantilized, Americanized, homogenized, sentimentalized; falsified, kitschified, and, in fact, blatantly and arrogantly denied. Among the falsifiers have been dramatists and directors, translators and litigators, Anne Frank's own father, and even—or especially—the public, both readers and theatregoers, all over the world. A deeply truth-telling work has been turned into an instrument of partial truth, surrogate truth, or anti-truth. The pure has been made impure—sometimes in the name of the reverse. Almost every hand that has approached the diary with the well-meaning intention of publicizing it has contributed to the subversion of history.

The diary is taken to be a Holocaust document; that is overridingly what it is not. Nearly every edition—and there have been innumerable editions—is emblazoned with words like "a song to life" or "a poignant delight in the infinite human spirit." Such characterizations rise up in the bitter perfume of mockery. A song to life? The diary is incomplete, truncated, broken off—or, rather, it is completed by Westerbork (the hellish transit camp in Holland from which Dutch Jews were deported), and by Auschwitz, and by the fatal winds of Bergen-Belsen. It is here, and not in the "secret annex," that the crimes we have come to call the Holocaust were enacted. Our entry into those crimes begins with columns of numbers: the meticulous lists of deportations, in handsome bookkeepers' handwriting, starkly set down in German "transport books." From these columns—headed, like goods for export, *"Ausgangs-Transporte nach dem Osten"* (outgoing shipments to the east)—it is possible to learn that Anne Frank and the others were moved to Auschwitz on the night of September 6, 1944, in a collection of a thousand and nineteen *Stücke* (or "pieces," another commodities term). That same night, five hundred and forty-nine persons were gassed, including one from the Frank group (the father of Peter van Daan) and every child under fifteen. Anne, at fifteen, and seventeen-year-old Margot were spared, apparently for labor. The end of October, from the twentieth to the twenty-eighth, saw the gassing of more than six thousand human beings within two hours of their arrival, including a thousand boys eighteen and under. In December, two thousand and ninety-three female prisoners perished from starvation and exhaustion, in the women's camp; early in January, Edith Frank expired.

But Soviet forces were hurtling toward Auschwitz, and in November the order went out to conceal all evidences of gassing and to blow up the crematoria. Tens of thousands of inmates, debilitated and already near extinction, were driven out in bitter cold on death marches. Many were shot. In an evacuation that occurred either on October 28th or on November 2nd, Anne and Margot were dispatched to Bergen-Belsen. Margot was the first to succumb. A survivor recalled that she fell dead to the ground from the wooden slab on which she lay, eaten by lice, and that Anne, heartbroken and skeletal, naked under a bit of rag, died a day or two later.

To come to the diary without having earlier assimilated Elie Wiesel's "Night" and Primo Levi's "The Drowned and the Saved" (to mention two witnesses only), or the columns of figures in the transport books, is to allow oneself to stew in an implausible and ugly innocence. The litany of blurbs— "a lasting testament to the indestructible nobility of the human spirit," "an everlasting source of courage and inspiration"—is no more substantial than any other display of self-delusion. The success—the triumph—of Bergen-Belsen was precisely that it blotted out the possibility of courage, that it proved to be a lasting testament to the human spirit's easy destructibility. "*Hier ist kein Warum*," a guard at Auschwitz warned: here there is no "why," neither question nor answer, only the dark of unreason. Anne Frank's story, truthfully told, is unredeemed and unredeemable.

These are notions that are hard to swallow—so they have not been swallowed. There are some, bored beyond toleration and callous enough to admit it, who are sick of hearing—yet again!—about depredations fifty years gone. "These old events," one of these fellows may complain, "can rake you over only so much. If I'm going to be lashed, I might as well save my skin for more recent troubles in the world." (I quote from a private letter from a distinguished author.) The more common response respectfully discharges an obligation to pity: it is dutiful. Or it is sometimes less than dutiful. It is sometimes frivolous, or indifferent, or presumptuous. But what even the most exemplary sympathies are likely to evade is the implacable recognition that Auschwitz and Bergen-Belsen, however sacramentally prodded, can never yield light.

The vehicle that has most powerfully accomplished this almost universal obtuseness is Anne Frank's diary. In celebrating Anne Frank's years in the secret annex, the nature and meaning of her death has been, in effect, forestalled. The diary's keen lens is helplessly opaque to the diarist's explicit doom—and this opacity, replicated in young readers in particular, has led to shamelessness.

It is the shamelessness of appropriation. Who owns Anne Frank? The children of the world, say the sentimentalists. A case in point is the aston- ishing correspondence, published in 1995 under the title "Love, Otto," between Cara Wilson, a Californian born in 1944, and Otto Frank, the father of Anne Frank. Wilson, then twelve-year-old Cara Weiss, was invited by Twentieth Century Fox to audition for the part of Anne in a projected film version of the diary. "I didn't get the part," the middle-aged Wilson writes, "but by now I had found a whole new world. Anne Frank's diary, which I read and reread, spoke to me and my dilemmas, my anxieties, my secret passions. She felt the way I did . . . I identified so strongly with this eloquent girl of my own age, that I now think I sort of became her in my own mind." And on

what similarities does Wilson rest her acute sense of identification with a
hunted child in hiding?

> I was miserable being me. . . . I was on the brink of that awful
> abyss of teenagedom and I, too, needed someone to talk to. . . .
> (Ironically, Anne, too, expressed a longing for more attention
> from her father.) . . . Dad's whole life was a series of meetings. At
> home, he was too tired or too frustrated to unload on. I had
> something else in common with Anne. We both had to share
> with sisters who were prettier and smarter than we felt we were.
> . . . despite the monumental differences in our situations, to this
> day I feel that Anne helped me get through the teens with a sense
> of inner focus. She spoke for me. She was strong for me. She had
> so much hope when I was ready to call it quits.

A sampling of Wilsons' concerns as she matured appears in the interstices
of her exchanges with Otto Frank, which, remarkably, date from 1959 until his
death, in 1980. For instance: "The year was 1968—etched in my mind. I can't
ever forget it. Otis Redding was 'Sittin' on the Dock of the Bay' . . . while we
hummed along to 'Hey Jude' by the Beatles." "In 1973–74," she reports, "I was
wearing headbands, pukka-shell necklaces, and American Indian anything.
Tattoos were a rage"—but enough. Tattoos were the rage, she neglects to recall,
in Auschwitz; and the Auschwitz survivor who was her patient correspondent
for more than two decades, Wilson remarks, "Well, what choice did the poor
man have? Whenever an attack of 'I-can't-take-this-any-longer' would hit me,
I'd put it all into lengthy diatribes to my distant guru, Otto Frank."

That the designated guru replied, year after year, to embarrassing and
shabby effusions like these may open a new pathway into our generally
obscure understanding of the character of Otto Frank. His responses—from
Basel, where he had settled with his second wife—were consistently attentive, formal, kindly. When Wilson gave birth, he sent her a musical toy, and
he faithfully offered a personal word about her excitements as she supplied
them: her baby sons, her dance lessons, her husband's work on commercials,
her freelance writing. But his letters were also political and serious. It is
good, he wrote in October, 1970, to take "an active part in trying to abolish
injustices and all sorts of grievances, but we cannot follow your views
regarding the Black Panthers." And in December, 1973, "As you can
imagine, we were highly shocked about the unexpected attack of the Arabs
on Israel on Yom Kippur and are now mourning with all those who lost
members of their families." Presumably he knew something about losing a
family. Wilson, insouciantly sliding past these faraway matters, was otherwise
preoccupied, "finding our little guys sooo much fun."

The unabashed trifling of Cara Wilson—whose "identification" with Anne Frank can be duplicated by the thousand, though she may be more audacious than most—point to a conundrum. Never mind that the intellectual distance between Wilson and Anne Frank is immeasurable; not every self-conscious young girl will be a prodigy. Did Otto Frank not comprehend that Cara Wilson was deaf to everything the loss of his daughter represented? Did he not see, in Wilson's letters alone, how a denatured approach to the diary might serve to promote amnesia of what was rapidly turning into history? A protected domestic space, however threatened and endangered, can, from time to time, mimic ordinary life. The young who are encouraged to embrace the diary cannot always be expected to feel the difference between the mimicry and the threat. And (like Cara Wilson) most do not. Natalie Portman, sixteen years old, who will debut as Anne Frank in the roadway revival this December of the famous play based on the diary—a play that has itself influenced the way the diary is read—concludes from her own reading that "it's funny, it's hopeful, and she's a happy person."

Otto Frank, it turns out, is complicit in this shallowly upbeat view. Again and again, in every conceivable context, he had it as his aim to emphasize "Anne's idealism" "Anne's spirit," almost never calling attention to how and why that idealism and spirit were smothered, and unfailingly generalizing the sources of hatred. If the child is father of the man—if childhood shapes future sensibility—then Otto Frank, despite his sufferings in Auschwitz, may have had less in common with his own daughter than he was ready to recognize. As the diary gained publication in country after country, its renown accelerating year by year, he spoke not merely about but for its author—and who, after all, would have a greater right? The surviving father stood in for the dead child, believing that his words would honestly represent hers. He was scarcely entitled to such certainty: fatherhood does not confer surrogacy.

Otto Frank's own childhood, in Frankfurt, Germany, was wholly unclouded. A banker's son, he lived untrammelled until the rise of the Nazi regime, when he was already forty-four. At nineteen, in order to acquire training in business, he went to New York with Nathan Straus, a fellow-student and an heir to the Macy's department-store fortune. During the First World War, Frank was an officer in the German military, and in 1925 he married Edith Holländer, a manufacturer's daughter. Margot was born in 1926 and Anneliese Marie, called Anne, in 1929. His characteristically secular world view belonged to an era of quiet assimilation, or, more accurately, accommodation (which includes a modicum of deference), when German Jews had become, at least in their own minds, well integrated into German society. From birth, Otto Frank had breathed the free air of the affluent bourgeoisie.

Anne's childhood, by contrast, fell into shadows almost immediately. She was not yet four when the German persecutions of Jews began, and from then until the anguished close of her days she lived as a refugee and a victim. In 1933, the family fled from Germany to Holland, where Frank had commercial connections, and where he established a pectin business. By 1940, the Germans had occupied the Netherlands. In Amsterdam, Jewish children, Anne among them, were thrown out of the public-school system and made to wear the yellow star. At thirteen, on November 19, 1942, already in hiding, Anne Frank could write:

> In the evenings when it's dark, I often see long lines of good, innocent people accompanied by crying children, walking on and on, ordered about by a handful of men who bully and beat them until they nearly drop. No one is spared. The sick, the elderly, children, babies, and pregnant women—all are marched to their death.

And earlier, on October 9th, after hearing the report of an escape from Westerbork:

> Our many Jewish friends and acquaintances are being taken away in droves. The Gestapo is treating them very roughly and transporting them in cattle cars to Westerbork. . . . The people get almost nothing to eat, much less to drink, as water is available only one hour a day, and there's only one toilet and sink for several thousand people. Men and women sleep in the same room, and women and children often have their heads shaved. . . . If it's that bad in Holland, what must it be like in those faraway and uncivilized places where the Germans are sending them? We assume that most of them are being murdered. The English radio says they're being gassed.

Perhaps not even a father is justified in thinking he can distill the "ideas" of this alert and sorrowing child, with scenes such as these inscribed in her psyche, and with the desolations of Auschwitz and Bergen-Belsen still ahead. His preference was to accentuate what he called Anne's "optimistic view on life." Yet the diary's most celebrated line (infamously celebrated, one might add)—"I still believe, in spite of everything, that people are truly good at heart"—has been torn out of its bed of thorns. Two sentences later (and three weeks before she was seized and shipped to Westerbork), the diarist sets down a vision of darkness:

I see the world being slowly transformed into a wilderness, I hear the approaching thunder that, one day, will destroy us too, I feel the suffering of millions. . . . In the meantime, I must hold on to my ideals. Perhaps the day will come when I'll be able to realize them!

Because that day never came, both Miep Gies, the selflessly courageous woman who devoted herself to the sustenance of those in hiding, and Hannah Goslar, Anne's Jewish schoolmate and the last to hear her tremulous cries in Bergen-Belsen, objected to Otto Frank's emphasis on the diary's "truly good at heart" utterance. That single sentence has become, universally, Anne Frank's message, virtually her motto—whether or not such a credo could have survived the camps. Why should this sentence be taken as emblematic, and not, for example, another? "There's a destructive urge in people, the urge to rage, murder, and kill," Anne wrote on May 3, 1944, pondering the spread of guilt. These are words that do not soften, ameliorate, or give the lie to the pervasive horror of her time. Nor do they pull the wool over the eyes of history.

Otto Frank grew up with a social need to please his environment and not to offend it; that was the condition of entering the mainstream, a bargain German Jews negotiated with themselves. It was more dignified, and safer, to praise than to blame. Far better, then, in facing the larger postwar world that the diary had opened to him, to speak of goodness rather than destruction: so much of that larger world had participated in the urge to rage. (The diary notes how Dutch anti-Semitism, "to our great sorrow and dismay," was increasing even as the Jews were being hauled away.) After the liberation of the camps, the heaps of emaciated corpses were accusation enough. Postwar sensibility hastened to migrate elsewhere, away from the cruel and the culpable. It was a tone and a mood that affected the diary's reception; it was a mood and a tone that, with cautious yet crucial excisions, the diary itself could be made to support. And so the diarist's dread came to be described as hope, her terror as courage, her prayers of despair as inspiring. And since the diary was now defined as a Holocaust document, the perception of the cataclysm itself was being subtly accommodated to espressions like "man's inhumanity to man," diluting and befogging specific historical events and their motives. "We must not flog the past," Frank insisted in 1969. His concrete response to the past was the establishment, in 1957, of the Anne Frank Foundation and its offshoot the International Youth Center, situated in the Amsterdam house where the diary was composed, to foster "as many contacts as possible between young people of different nationalities, races and religions"—a civilized and tenderhearted goal that nevertheless washed away into do-gooder abstraction the explicit urge to rage that had devoured his daughter.

Otto Frank was merely an accessory to the transformation of the diary from one kind of witness to another kind: from the painfully revealing to the partially concealing. If Anne Frank has been made into what we nowadays call an "icon," it is because of the Pulitzer Prize–winning play derived from the diary—a play that rapidly achieved worldwide popularity, and framed the legend even the newest generation has come to believe in. Adapted by Albert Hackett and Frances Goodrich, a Hollywood husband-and-wife screen-writing team, the theatricalized version opened on Broadway in 1955, ten years after the end of the war, and its portrayal of the "funny, hopeful, happy" Anne continues to reverberate, not only in how the diary is construed but in how the Holocaust itself is understood. The play was a work born in contro-versy, destined to roil on and on in rancor and litigation. Its tangle of contending lawyers finally came to resemble nothing so much as the knotted imbroglio of Jarndyce vs. Jarndyce, the unending court case of *Bleak House*. Many of the chief figures in the protracted conflict over the Hacketts' play have by now left the scene, but the principal issues, far from fading away, have, after so many decades, intensified. Whatever the ramifications of these issues, whatever perspectives they illumine or defy, the central question stands fast: Who owns Anne Frank?

The hero, or irritant (depending on which side of the controversy one favors), in the genesis of the diary's dramatization was Meyer Levin, a Chicago-born novelist of the social-realist school, the author of such fairly successful works as *The Old Bunch, Complusion*, and *The Settlers*. Levin began as a man of the left, though a strong anti-Stalinist: he was drawn to prole-tarian fiction ("Citizens," about steelworkers), and had gone to Spain in the thirties to report on the Civil War. In 1945, as a war correspondent attached to the Fourth Armored Division, he was among the first Americans to enter Buchenwald, Dachau, and Begen-Belsen. What he saw there was ungras-pable and unendurable. "As I groped in the first weeks, beginning to appre-hend the monstrous shape of the story I would have to tell," he wrote, "I knew already that I would never penetrate its heart of bile, for the magnitude of this horror seemed beyond human register." The truest telling, he affirmed, would have to rise up out of the mouth of a victim.

His "obsession," as he afterward called it—partly in mockery of the opposition his later views evoked—had its beginning in those repeated scenes of piled-up bodies as he investigated camp after camp. From then on, he could be said to carry the mark of Abel. He dedicated himself to helping the survivors get to Mandate Palestine, a goal that Britain had made illegal. In 1946, he reported from Tel Aviv on the uprising against British rule, and during the next two years he produced a pair of films on the struggles of the survivors to reach Palestine. In 1950, he published "In Search," an examination of the effects of the European cataclysm on his experience and sensibility as an American Jew. (Thomas Mann acclaimed the book as "a human document of high order, written by a witness of our fantastic epoch whose gaze remained both clear and steady.") Levin's intensifying focus on the Jewish condition in the twentieth century grew more and more heated, and when his wife, the novelist Tereska Torres, handed him the French edition of the diary (it had previously appeared only in Dutch) he felt he had found what he had thirsted after: a voice crying up from the ground, an authentic witness to the German onslaught.

He acted instantly. He sent Otto Frank a copy of "In Search" and in effect offered his services as an unofficial agent to secure British and American publication, asserting his distance from any financial gain; his interest, he said, was purely "one of sympathy." He saw in the diary the possibility of "a very touching play or film," and asked Frank's permission to explore the idea. Frank at first avoided reading Levin's book, saturated as it was in passions and commitments so foreign to his own susceptibilities. He was not unfamiliar with Levin's preoccupations; he had seen and liked one of his films. He encouraged Levin to go ahead—though a dramatization, he observed, would perforce "be rather different from the real contents" of the diary. Hardly so, Levin protested: no compromise would be needed; all the diarist's thoughts could be preserved.

The "real contents" had already been altered by Frank himself, and understandably, given the propriety of his own background and of the times. The diary contained, here and there, intimate adolescent musings, talk of how contraceptives work, and explicit anatomical description: "In the upper part, between the outer labia, there is a fold of skin that, on second thought, looks like a kind of blister. That's the clitoris. Then come the inner labia . . . " All this Frank edited out. He also omitted passages recording his daughter's angry resistance to the nervous fussiness of her mother ("the most rotten person in the world"). Undoubtedly he better understood Edith Frank's protective tremors, and was unwilling to perpetuate a negative portrait. Beyond this, he deleted numerous expressions of religious faith, a direct reference to Yom Kippur, terrified reports of Germans seizing Jews in Amsterdam. It was prudence, prudishness, and perhaps his own deracinated temperament that stimulated many of these tamperings. In 1991, eleven years after Frank's death, a "definitive edition" of the diary restored everything he had expurgated. But the image of Anne Frank as merry innocent and steadfast idealist—an image the play vividly promoted—was by then ineradicable.

A subsequent bowdlerization, in 1950, was still more programmatic, and crossed over even more seriously into the area of Levin's concern for uncompromised faithfulness. The German edition's translator, Anneliese Schütz, in order to mask or soft-pedal German culpability, went about methodically blurring every hostile reference to Germans and German. Anne's parodic list of house rules, for instance, included "*Use of language:* It is necessary to speak softly at all times. Only the language of civilized people may be spoken, thus no German." The German translation reads, "*Alle Kultur-sprachen . . . aber leise!*"—"all civilized languages . . . but softly!" "Heroism in the war or when confronting the Germans" is dissolved into "heroism in the war and in the struggle against oppression." ("A book intended after all for sale in Germany," Schütz explained, "cannot abuse the Germans.") The diarist's honest cry, in the midst of a vast persecution, that "there is no greater hostility than exists between Germans and Jews" became, in Schütz's version, "there is no greater hostility in the world than between these Germans and Jews!" Frank agreed to the latter change because, he said, it was what his daughter had really meant: she "by no means measured all Germans by the same yardstick. For, as she knew so well, even in those days we had many good friends among the Germans." But this guarded accommodationist view is Otto Frank's own; it is nowhere in the diary. Even more striking than Frank's readiness to accede to such misrepresentations is the fact that for forty-one years (until a more accurate translation appeared) no reader of the diary in German had ever known an intact text.

In contemplating a dramatization and pledging no compromise, Levin told Frank he would do it "tenderly and with utmost fidelity." He was clear about what he meant by fidelity. In his eyes the diary was conscious testimony to Jewish faith and suffering; and it was this, and this nearly alone, that defined for him its psychological, historical, and metaphysical genuineness, and its significance for the world. With these convictions foremost, Levin went in search of a theatrical producer. At the same time, he was unflagging in pressing for publication; but the work was meanwhile slowly gaining independent notice. Janet Flanner, in her "Letter from Paris" in *The New Yorker* of November 11, 1950, noted the French publication of a book by "a precocious, talented little Frankfurt Jewess"—apparently oblivious of the unpleasant echoes, post-Hitler, of "Jewess." Sixteen English-language publishers on both sides of the Atlantic had already rejected the diary when Levin succeeded in placing it with Valentine Mitchell, a London firm. His negotiations with a Boston house were still incomplete when Doubleday came forward to secure publication rights directly from Frank. Relations between Levin and Frank were, as usual, warm; Frank repeatedly thanked Levin for his efforts to further the fortunes of the diary, and Levin continued under the impression that Frank would support him as the playwright of choice.

If a front-page review in the *New York Times Book Review* can rocket a book to instant sanctity, that is what Meyer Levin, in the spring of 1952, achieved for "Anne Frank: The Diary of a Young Girl." It was an assignment he had gone after avidly. Barbara Zimmerman (afterward Barbara Epstein, a founder of *The New York Review of Books*), the diary's young editor at Doubleday, had earlier recognized its potential as "a minor classic," and had enlisted Eleanor Roosevelt to supply an introduction. (According to Levin, it was ghostwritten by Zimmerman.) Levin now joined Zimmerman and Doubleday in the project of choosing a producer. Doubleday was to take over as Frank's official agent, with the stipulation that Levin would have an active hand in the adaptation. "I think that I can honestly say," Levin wrote Frank, "that I am as well qualified as any other writer for this particular task." In a cable to Doubleday, Frank appeared to agree: "DESIRE LEVIN AS WRITER OR COLLABORATOR IN ANY TREATMENT TO GUARANTEE IDEA OF BOOK." The catch, it would develop, lurked in a perilous contingency: Whose idea? Levin's? Frank's? The producer's? The director's? In any case, Doubleday was already doubtful about Levin's ambiguous role: What if an interested producer decided on another playwright?

What happened next—an avalanche of furies and recriminations lasting years—has lately become the subject of a pair of arresting discussions of the Frank-Levin affair. And if "affair" suggests an event on the scale of the Dryefus case, that is how Levin saw it: as an unjust stripping away of his rightful position, with implications far beyond his personal predicament. *An Obsession with Anne Frank*, by Lawrence Graver, published by the University of California Press in 1995, is the first study to fashion a coherent narrative out of the welter of claims, counterclaims, letters, cables, petitions, polemics, and rumbling confusions which accompany any examination of the diary's journey to the stage. *The Stolen Legacy of Anne Frank*, by Ralph Melnick, out just now from Yale, is denser in detail and in sources than its predecessor, and more insistent in tone. Both are accomplished works of scholarship that converge on the facts and diverge in their conclusions. Graver is reticent with his sympathies; Melnick is Levin's undisguised advocate. Graver finds no villains; Melnick finds Lillian Hellman.

Always delicately respectful of Frank's dignity and rights—and always mindful of the older man's earlier travail—Levin had promised that he would step aside if a more prominent playwright, someone "world famous," should appear. Stubbornly and confidently, he went on toiling over his own version. As a novelist, he was under suspicion of being unable to write drama. (In after years, when he had grown deeply bitter, he listed, in retaliation, "Sartre, Gorky, Galsworthy, Steinbeck, Wilder!") Though there are many extant drafts of Levin's play, no definitive script is available; both publication and performance were proscribed by Franks' attorneys. A script staged without authorization by the Israel Soldiers' Theatre in 1966 sometimes passes from hand to hand, and reads well: moving, theatrical, actable, professional. This later work was not, however, the script submitted in the summer of 1952 to Cheryl Crawford, one of a number of Broadway producers who rushed in with bids in the wake of the diary's acclaim. Crawford, an eminent co-founder of the Actors Studio, initially encouraged Levin, offering him first consideration and, if his script was not entirely satisfactory, the aid of a more experienced collaborator. Then—virtually overnight—she rejected his draft outright. Levin was bewildered and infuriated, and from then on he became an intractable and indefatigable warrior on behalf of his play—and on behalf, he contended, of the diary's true meaning. In his *Times* review he had summed it up stirringly as the voice of "six million vanished Jewish souls."

Doubleday, meanwhile, sensing complications ahead, had withdrawn as Frank's theatrical agent, finding Levin's presence—injected by Frank—too intrusive, too maverick, too independent and entrepreneurial: fixed, they believed, only on his own interest, which was to stick to his insistence on the superiority of his work over all potential contenders. Frank, too, had begun—kindly, politely, and with tireless assurances of his gratitude to Levin—to move closer to Doubleday's cooler views, especially as urged by Barbara Zimmerman. She was twenty-four years old, the age Anne would have been, very intelligent and attentive. Adoring letters flowed back and forth between them, Frank addressing her as "little Barbara" and "dearest little one." On one occasion he gave her an antique gold pin. About Levin, Zimmerman finally concluded that he was "impossible to deal with in any terms, officially, legally, morally, personally"—a "compulsive neurotic . . . destroying both himself and Anne's play." (There was, of course, no such entity as "Anne's play.")

What had caused Crawford to change her mind so precipitately? She had given Levin's script for further consideration to Lillian Hellman and to the producers Robert Whitehead and Kermit Bloomgarden. All were theatre luminaries; all spurned Levin's work. Frank's confidence in Levin, already much diminished, failed altogether. Advised by Doubleday, he put his trust in the Broadway professionals, while Levin fought on alone. Famous names—Maxwell Anderson, John Van Druten, Carson McCullers—came and went. Crawford herself ultimately pulled out, fearing a lawsuit by Levin. In the end—with the vigilant Levin still agitating loudly and publicly for the primacy of his work—Kermit Bloomgarden surfaced as a producer and Garson Kanin as director. Hellman had recommended Bloomgarden; she had also recommended Frances Goodrich and Albert Hackett. The Hacketts had a long record of Hollywood hits, from "Father of the Bride" to "It's a Wonderful Life," and they had successfully scripted a series of lighthearted musicals. Levin was appalled—had his sacred vision been pushed aside not for the awaited world-famous dramatist but for a pair of frivolous screen drudges, mere "hired hands"?

The hired hands were earnest and reverent. They began at once to read up on European history, Judaism, and Jewish practice; they consulted a rabbi. They corresponded eagerly with Frank, looking to satisfy his expectations. They traveled to Amsterdam and visited 263 Prinsengracht, the house on the canal where the Franks, the van Daans, and Dussel had been hidden. They met Johannes Kleiman, who, together with Victor Kugler and Miep Gies, had taken over the management of Frank's business in order to conceal and protect him and his family in the house behind. Reacting to the Hacketts' lifelong remoteness from Jewish subject matter, Levin took out an ad in the New York *Post* attacking Bloomgarden and asking that his play be given a hearing. "My work," he wrote, "has been with the Jewish story. I tried to dramatize the *Diary* as Anne would have, in her own words. . . . I feel my work has earned the right to be judged by you, the public." "Ridiculous and laughable," said Bloomgarden. Appealing to the critic Brooks Atkinson, Levin complained—extravagantly, outrageously—that his play was being "killed by the same arbitrary disregard that brought an end to Anne and six million others." Frank stopped answering Levin's letters; many he returned unopened.

The Hacketts, too, in their earliest drafts, were devotedly "with the Jewish story." Grateful to Hellman for getting them the job, and crushed by Bloomgardens' acute dislike of their efforts so far, they flew to Martha's Vineyard weekend after weekend to receive advice from Hellman. "She was amazing," Goodrich crowed, happy to comply. Hellman's slant—and that of Bloomgarden and Kanin—was consistently in a direction opposed to Levin's. Where the diary touched on Anne's consciousness of Jewish fate or faith, they quietly erased the reference or change its emphasis. Whatever was specific they made generic. The sexual tenderness between Anne and the young Peter van Daan was moved to the forefront. Comedy overwhelmed darkness. Anne became an all-American girl, an echo of the perky character in "Junior Miss," a popular play of the previous decade. The Zionist aspirations of Margot, Anne's sister, disappeared. The one liturgical note, a Hanukkah ceremony, was absurdly defined in terms of local contemporary habits ("eight days of presents"); a jolly jingle replaced the traditional "Rock of Ages," with its sombre allusions to historic travail. (Kanin had insisted on something "spirited and gay," so as not to give "the wrong feeling entirely." "Hebrew," he argued, "would simply alienate the audience.")

Astonishingly, the Nazified notion of "race" leaped out in a line attributed to Hellman and nowhere present in the diary. "We're not the only people that've had to suffer," the Hacketts' Anne says. "There've always been people that've had to . . . sometimes one race . . . sometimes another." This pallid speech, yawning with vagueness, was conspicuously opposed to the pivotal reflection it was designed to betray:

> In the eyes of the world, we're doomed, but if after all this suffering, there are still Jews left, the Jewish people will be held up as an example. Who know, maybe our religion will teach the world and all the people in it about goodness, and that's the reason, the only reason, we have to suffer. . . . God has never deserted our people. Through the ages Jews have had to suffer, but through the ages they've gone on living, and the centuries of suffering have only made them stronger.

For Kanin, this kind of rumination was "an embarrassing piece of special pleading. . . . The fact that in this play the symbols of persecution and oppression are Jews is incidental, and Anne, in stating the argument so, reduces her magnificent stature." And so it went throughout. The particularized plight of Jews in hiding was vaporized into what Kanin called "the infinite." Reality—the diary's central condition—was "incidental." The passionately contemplative child, brooding on concrete evil, was made into an emblem of evasion. Her history had a habitation and a name; the infinite was nameless and nowhere.

For Levin, the source and first cause of these excisions was Lillian Hellman. Hellman, he believed, had "supervised" the Hacketts, and Hellman was fundamentally political and inflexibly doctrinaire. Her outlook lay at the root of a conspiracy. She was an impenitent Stalinist; she followed, he said, the Soviet line. Like the Soviets, she was anti-Zionist. And, just as the Soviets had obliterated Jewish particularity at Babi Yar, the ravine where thousands of Jews, shot by the Germans, lay unnamed and effaced in their deaths, so Hellman had directed the Hacketts to blur the identity of the characters in the play.

The sins of the Soviets and the sins of Hellman and her Broadway deputies were, in Levin's mind, identical. He set out to punish the man who had allowed all this to come to pass: Otto Frank had allied himself with the pundits of erasure; Otto Frank had stood aside when Levin's play was elbowed out of the way. What recourse remained for a man so affronted and injured? Meyer Levin sued Otto Frank. It was as if, someone observed, a suit were being brought against the father of Joan of Arc. The bulky snarl of courtroom arguments resulted in small satisfaction for Levin: because the structure of the Hacketts' play was in some ways similar to his, the jury detected plagiarism; yet even this limited triumph foundered on the issue of damages. Levin sent out broadsides, collected signatures, summoned a committee of advocacy, lectured from pulpits, took out ads, rallied rabbis and writers (Norman Mailer among them). He wrote "The Obsession," his grandly confessional "J'Accuse," rehearsing, in skirmish after skirmish, his fight for the staging of his own adaptation. In return, furious charges flew at him: he was a red-baiter, a McCarthyite. The term "paranoid" began to circulate. Why rant against the popularization and dilution that was Broadway's lifeblood? "I certainly have no wish to inflict depression on an audience," Kanin had argued. "I don't consider that a legitimate theatrical end." (So much for "Hamlet" and "King Lear.")

Grateful for lightness, reviewers agreed. What they came away from was the charm of Susan Strasberg as a radiant Anne, and Joseph Schildkraut in the role of a wise and steadying Otto Frank, whom the actor engagingly resembled. "Anne is not going to her death; she is going to leave a dent on life, and let death take what's left," Walter Kerr, on a mystical note, wrote in the *Herald Tribune*. *Variety* seemed relieved that the play avoided "hating the Nazis, hating what they did to millions of innocent people," and instead came off as "glowing, moving, frequently humorous," with "just about every-thing one could wish for. It is not grim." The *Daily News* confirmed what Kanin had striven for: "Not in any important sense a Jewish play. . . . Anne Frank is a Little Orphan Annie brought into vibrant life." Audiences laughed and were charmed; but were also dazed and moved.

And audiences multiplied: the Hacketts' drama went all over the world—including Israel, where numbers of survivors were remaking their lives—and was everywhere successful. The play's reception in Germany was especially noteworthy. In an impressive and thorough-going essay entitled "Popularization and Memory," Alvin Rosenfeld, a professor of English at Indiana University, recounts the development of the Anne Frank phenom-enon in the country of her birth. "The theater reviews of the time," Rosen-feld reports, "tell of audiences sitting in stunned silence at the play and leaving the performance unable to speak or look one another in the eye." These were self-conscious and thin-skinned audiences; in the Germany of the fifties, theatregoers still belonged to the generation of the Nazi era. (On Broadway, Kanin had unblinkingly engaged Gusti Huber, of that same generation, to play Anne Frank's mother. As a member of the Nazi Actors Guild until Germany's defeat, Huber had early on disparaged "non-Aryan artists.") But the strange muteness in theatres may have derived not so much from guilt or shame as from an all-encompassing compassion; or call it self-pity. "We see in Anne Frank's fate," a German drama critic offered, "our own fate—the tragedy of human existence per se." Hannah Arendt, philosopher and Hitler refugee, scorned such oceanic expressions, calling it "cheap sentimentality at the expense of a great catastrophe." And Bruno Bettelheim, a survivor of Dachau and Buchenwald, condemned the play's most touted line: "If all men are good, there was never an Auschwitz." A decade after the fall of Nazism, the spirited and sanitized young girl of the play became a vehicle for German communal identification—with the victim, not the persecutors—and, according to Rosenfeld, a continuing "symbol of moral and intellectual convenience." The Anne Frank whom thousands saw in seven openings in seven cities "spoke affirmatively about life and not accusingly about her torturers." No German in uniform appeared onstage. "In a word," Rosenfeld concludes, "Anne Frank has become a ready-at-hand formula for easy forgiveness."

The mood of consolation lingers on, as Otto Frank meant it to—and not only in Germany, where, even after fifty years, the issue is touchiest. Sanctified and absolving, shorn of darkness, Anne Frank remains in all countries a revered and comforting figure in the contemporary mind. In Japan, because both diary and play mention first menstruation, "Anne Frank" has become a code word among teen-agers for getting one's period. In Argentina in the seventies, church publications began to link her with Roman Catholic martyrdom. "Commemoration," the French cultural critic Tzvetan Todorov explains, "is always the adaptation of memory to the needs of today."

But there is a note that drills deeper than commemoration: it goes to the idea of identification. To "identify with" is to become what one is not, to become what one is not is to usurp, to usurp is to own—and who, after all, in the half century since Miep Gies retrieved the scattered pages of the diary, really owns Anne Frank? Who can speak for her? Her father, who, after reading the diary and confessing that he "did not know" her, went on to tell us what he thought she meant? Meyer Levin, who claimed to be her authentic voice—so much so that he dared to equate the dismissal of his work, however ignobly motivated, with Holocaust annihilation? Hellman, Bloomgarden, Kanin, whose interpretations clung to a collective ideology of human interchangeability? (In discounting the significance of the Jewish element, Kanin had asserted that "people have suffered because of being English, French, German, Italian, Ethiopian, Mohammedan, Negro, and so on"—as if this were not all the more reason to comprehend and particularize each history.) And what of Cara Wilson and "the children of the world," who have reduced the persecution of a people to the trials of adolescence?

All these appropriations, whether cheaply personal or densely ideological, whether seen as exalting or denigrating, have contributed to the conversion of Anne Frank into usable goods. There is no authorized version other than the diary itself, and even this has been brought into question by the Holocaust-denial industry—in part a spin off of the Anne Frank industry—which labels the diary a forgery. One charge is that Otto Frank wrote it himself, to make money. (Scurrilities like these necessitated the issuance, in 1986, of a Critical Edition by the Netherlands State Institute for War Documentation, including forensic evidence of handwriting and ink—a defensive hence sorrowful volume.)

No play can be judged wholly from what is on the page; a play has evocative powers beyond the words. Still, the Hacketts' work, read today, is very much a conventionally well made Broadway product of the fifties, alternating comical beats with scenes of alarm, a love story with a theft, wisdom with buffoonery. The writing is skilled and mediocre, not unlike much of contemporary commercial theatre. Yet this is the play that electrified audiences everywhere, that became a reverential if robotlike film, and that—far more than the diary—invented the world's Anne Frank. Was it the play or was it the times? The upcoming revival of the Hacketts' dramatization—promising revisions incorporating passages Otto Frank deleted from the diary—will no doubt stimulate all the old quarrelsome issues yet again. But with the Second World War and the Holocaust receding, especially for the young, into distant fable—no different from tales, say, of Attila the Hun—the revival enters an environment psychologically altered from that of the 1955 production. At the same time, Holocaust scholarship—survivor memoirs, oral histories, wave after wave of fresh documentation and analysis—has increased prodigiously. At Harvard, for instance, under the rubric "reception studies," a young scholar named Alex Sagan, a relative of the late astronomer, is examining the ways Anne Frank has been transmuted into, among other cultural manifestations, a heavenly body. And Steven Spielberg's "Schindler's List," about a Nazi industrialist as savior, has left its mark.

It may be, though, that a new production, even now, and even with cautious additions, will be heard in the play's original voice. It was always a voice of good will; it meant, as we say, well—and, financially, it certainly did well. But it was Broadway's style of good will, and that, at least for Meyer Levin, had the scent of ill. For him, and signally for Bloomgarden and Kanin, the most sensitive point—the focus of trouble—lay in the ancient dispute between the particular and the universal. All that was a distraction from the heart of the matter: in a drama about hiding, evil was hidden. And if the play remains essentially as the Hacketts wrote it, the likelihood is that Anne Frank's real history will hardly prevail over what was experienced, forty years ago, as history transcended, ennobled, rarefied. The first hint is already in the air, puffed by the play's young lead: *It's funny, it's hopeful, and she's a happy person.*

Evisceration, an elegy for the murdered. Evisceration by blurb and stage, by shrewdness and naïveté, by cowardice and spirituality, by forgiveness and indifference, by success and money, by vanity and rage, by principle and passion, by surrogacy and affinity. Evisceration by fame, by shame, by blame. By uplift and transcendence. By usurpation.

On Friday, August 4, 1944, the day of the arrest, Miep Gies climbed the stairs to the hiding place and found it ransacked and wrecked. The beleagured little band had been betrayed by an informer who was paid seven and a half guilders—about a dollar—for each person: sixty guilders for the lot. Miep Gies picked up what she recognized as Anne's papers and put them away, unread, in her desk drawer. There the diary lay untouched, until Otto Frank emerged alive from Auschwitz. "Had I read it, she said afterward, "I would have had to burn the diary because it would have been too dangerous for people about whom Anne had written." It was Miep Gies—the uncommon heroine of this story, a woman profoundly good, a failed savior— who succeeded in rescuing an irreplaceable masterwork. It may be shocking to think this (I am shocked as I think it), but one can imagine a still more salvational outcome: Anne Frank's diary burned, vanished, lost—saved from a world that made of it all things, some of them true, while floating lightly over the heavier truth of named and inhabited evil.

Chronology

1929   Annelies Marie (Anne) Frank born on June 12 in Frankfurt am Main, the daughter of Otto Frank and Edith Hollander Frank. Her older sister, Margot Betti, was born February 16, 1926.

1933   Summer. After the Nazis win municipal elections in Frankfurt, Otto Frank decides to emigrate with his family to the Netherlands, a neutral country, where he opens a branch of his brother-in-law's company, the Dutch Opekta Company, in Amsterdam. Edith and Margot join him in December; the family resides in an apartment at 378 Merwedeplein. Anne remains in Aachen, Germany, with her maternal grandmother, joining her family in March 1934.

1939   Grandmother Rosa Stern Hollander flees Aachen and joins the family in Amsterdam.

1940   May. Germany invades the Netherlands and occupation begins. October 22. Nazis issue "Aryanization" decree that no Jew may own a business; Otto Frank cedes legal control of business interest to trusted employees and friends Jan Gies and Victor Kugler.

1941   September. Anne and other Jewish children no longer allowed to attend school with non-Jews. Anti-Jewish decrees increase and freedom of movement becomes increasingly restricted.

1942   January. Otto Frank tries to obtain emigration papers for the
              family; Grandmother Hollander dies.
              May. All Dutch Jews, age six and older, required to wear a
              yellow Star of David sewn to their clothing; mass arrests of
              Jews and mandatory service in German work camps becomes
              routine. Frank family prepares to go into hiding in annex of
              rooms above Otto Frank's office at 263 Prinsengracht;
              members of Opekta Company staff agree to help them.
              June 12. Anne celebrates thirteenth birthday; receives a note-
              book with a red and white checked cover; she begins the first
              of two extant diaries, dated June 12 to December 5, 1942.
              July 5. Margot receives notice that she will be deported to a
              Nazi work camp.
              July 6. Otto, Edith, Margot, and Anne move into the annex.
              July 13. Otto Frank's business associate, Herman Van Pels,
              moves into the annex with his wife and son, Peter. Anne will call
              them the van Daans in her diary.
              November 16. Friedrich Pfeffer, a dentist, moves into the
              annex. Anne will write about him as Mr. Dussel.

1943   December 22. Anne begins a new volume of her diaries, the
              first entry since December 5, 1942, indicating that one diary
              has been lost.

1944   March 28. An exiled Minister of the Dutch government in
              London, in a radio broadcast, asks for documents and accounts
              of the Dutch war experience; Anne confides to her diary, on
              May 11, that she will become a journalist and writer: "In any
              case, I want to publish a book entitled *Het Achterhuis* after the
              war. Whether I shall succeed or not, I cannot say, but my diary
              will be a great help."
              March 29. Last recorded entry, made on loose sheets of paper,
              of notes and stories for *Het Achterhuis*; other versions lost.
              May 20. Begins writing *Het Achterhuis* ("the house behind" or
              "the secret annex").
              August 4, 10:00 A.M. After an anonymous call, Nazi police and
              Dutch collaborators arrest the residents of the annex; remove
              all in a covered truck to Central Office for Jewish Emigration,
              then to Weteringschans Prison. Miep Gies retrieves Anne's
              papers and diaries from the annex and hides them.
              August 8. Frank family, the Van Pels family, and Pfeffer

removed to Westerbork transit camp.

September 3. On what will be the last Auschwitz-bound train from Westerbork, all transported to Auschwitz death camp in Poland, arriving September 5; Herman Van Pels put to death.

October 30. Anne and Margot transported from Auschwitz to Bergen-Belsen, near Hanover, Germany, where thousands die from starvation and epidemics.

December. Friedrich Pfeffer dies at Neuengamme concentration camp, Germany.

1945   January 6. Edith Frank dies of starvation at Auschwitz.

January 27. Russian troops liberate Auschwitz.

Peter Van Pels survives SS "death march" from Auschwitz, but dies May 2 (?) at Mauthausen concentration camp, Austria, three days before it is liberated.

March (?). Margot dies of typhus at Bergen-Belsen.

April (?). Anne, age 15, dies of typhus at Bergen-Belsen.

April 15, 1945. British troops liberate Bergen-Belsen.

May. The Netherlands is liberated; the war in Europe ends.

June 3. Otto Frank, the only survivor of the annex, returns to Amsterdam, hoping to find his daughters; Miep Gies gives him Anne's papers about a month later. Otto Frank copies and edits the diaries and papers, revising them to "the essentials," omitting what he believes offensive to the living, unkind to the dead, or of no interest. Because of the intimate nature of the diary, shocking at that time for Anne's comments upon politics, sexuality, and adults, no publisher will accept it. Otto Frank continues to seek a publisher in order to fulfill Anne's wish to be remembered as a writer.

1946   Jan Romein, Dutch historian and editor of the journal *De Nieuwe Stem*, reads Otto Frank's transcription of the diary and publishes an article praising it, "A Child's Voice," in *Het Parool*, April 3, 1946. "Fragments from the Diary of Anne Frank," heavily edited by Otto Frank at the request of the publishing house, appears in the summer issue of *De Nieuwe Stem*.

1947   Diary published, in Dutch, as *Het Achterhuis*. 150,000 copies soon followed by second printing.

1950   *Journal de Anne Frank* published in France. *Das Tagebuch der Anne*

Frank published in Germany.

1952   *The Diary of a Young Girl,* by Anne Frank, published in England
        and the United States, where it had previously been rejected by
        ten publishers.

1955   October 5. *The Diary of Anne Frank* produced for theater,
        premiers on Broadway; wins 1955 Pulitzer Prize for drama.

1956   October 1. *The Diary of Anne Frank* performed in Germany;
        November 27, in The Netherlands.

1957   *The Diary of Anne Frank* produced for film. Anne Frank Founda-
        tion established to preserve the annex, and to implement "the
        ideals bequeathed to the world in the Diary of Anne Frank."

1960   May 3. Anne Frank House opens as a museum and cultural
        center at 263 Prinsengracht, Amsterdam.

1977   Anne Frank Center U.S.A. opens in New York.

1980   August 19. Otto Frank dies in Basel, Switzerland, at age 91.

1997   December 4. *The Diary of Anne Frank,* a play by Wendy
        Kesselman, opens on Broadway.
        Anne Frank Zentrum (Center) opens in Berlin.
        More than twenty-four million copies of the diary have been sold
        and it has been translated into fifty-five languages.

Contributors

HAROLD BLOOM is Sterling Professor of Humanities at Yale University and Professor of English at the New York University Graduate School. His works include *The Anxiety of Influence* (1973), *Agon: Toward a Theory of Revisionism* (1982), *The American Religion* (1992), *The Western Canon* (1994), and *Shakespeare: The Invention of the Human* (1998). Professor Bloom is a 1985 MacArthur Foundation Award recipient and served as the Charles Eliot Norton Professor of Poetry at Harvard University in 1987–88. He is the editor of more than 30 anthologies, and general editor of several series of literary criticism published by Chelsea House.

BRUNO BETTELHEIM (1903–1990) was a controversial child psychologist and writer. Among his published works are *The Art of the Obvious* (1993), *A Good Enough Parent* (1982), *The Uses of Enchantment* (1976), and the *Children of the Dream: Communal Child Rearing and American Education* (1969).

BARBARA CHIARELLO teaches writing at the University of Texas at Arlington. Her essays have appeared in several journals, including *Utopian Studies*.

LAWRENCE L. LANGER is Emeritus Professor of English, Simmons College. He is a foremost scholar of the Holocaust whose works include *Art from the Ashes: A Holocaust Anthology* (1995); *The Ruins of Memory: Holocaust Testimonies* (1991), winner of the 1991 National Book Critics Circle

Award; *The Age of Atrocity: Death in Modern Literature* (1978), and *The Holocaust and the Literary Imagination* (1975).

YASMINE ERGAS is a feminist scholar and critic, and coauthor, with Laura Balbo, of the monograph *Women's Studies in Italy* (1982).

SANDER L. GILMAN is Henry R. Luce Professor of the Liberal Arts and Human biology at The University of Chicago and current President of the Modern Language Association. His works include *Seeing the Insane* (1996), *Franz Kafka, the Jewish Patient* (1995), *The Case of Sigmund Freud* (1994), *Freud, Race, and Gender* (1993), and *Anti-Semitism in Times of Crisis* (1991).

SYLVIA PATTERSON ISKANDER is former Professor of English at the University of Southwestern Louisiana. She is a scholar of children's literature from the eighteenth century to the present.

MOLLY MAGID HOAGLAND has published articles in the *Weekly Standard* and the *New England Review*.

CYNTHIA OZICK is the author of fifteen books. Her most recent works include the novels *The Puttermesser Papers* (1997) and *The Shawl* (1989); and two collections of essays, *Art and Ardor* (1987) and *Metaphor and Memory* (1989). She has won numerous awards for her fiction and essays, including four O. Henry Prizes and a Guggenheim Fellowship.

Bibliography

Adler, David. *Picture Book of Anne Frank*. New York: Holiday House, 1993.

Barnes, Ian. "Anne Frank Forty Years On," In *History Today* (March 1985): 48–50.

Chapkis, Wendy. "The Uncensored Anne Frank," In *Ms.* (October 1986): 79–80.

Cohen, Steven A. *Anne Frank in the World*. Amsterdam: Anne Frank Foundation, 1985.

Frank, Anne. *Dagboek Van Anne Frank: Het Achterhuis*. Amsterdam, The Netherlands: Contact, 1968.

———. *The Works of Anne Frank*. New York: Doubleday, 1959.

———. *Tales from the House Behind*. New York: Bantam, 1966. Paperback edition, New York: Washington Square Press, 1984.

———. *The Diary of a Young Girl*. New York: Simon & Schuster, 1972. (This edited version of the diary includes a Reader's Supplement.)

————. *The Diary of a Young Girl: The Definitive Edition*. New York: Doubleday, 1995. (This unedited version of the diary contains versions [a] and [b].)

———— . *Anne Frank's Tales from the Secret Annex*. Garden City, NY: Doubleday, 1983. (Contains short stories, essays, memoirs, and an unfinished novel; some previously published.)

Gies, Miep. *Anne Frank Remembered: The Story of the Woman Who Helped to Hide the Frank Family*. New York: Simon & Schuster, 1982.

Goodrich, Frances and Albert Hackett. *The Diary of Anne Frank* (play). New York: Random House, 1956.

Hurwitz, Johanna. *Anne Frank: Life in Hiding*. Philadephia: Jewish Publication Society, 1989.

Lindwer, Willy. *The Last Seven Months of Anne Frank*. New York: Pantheon Books, 1991.

Manheim, Ralph and Michel Mok, trans. *Anne Frank's Tales from the Secret Annex*. New York: Doubleday, 1984.

Pinsker, Sanford. "Marrying Anne Frank: Modernist Art, the Holocaust, and Mr. Philip Roth," In *Holocaust Studies Annual* 3 (1985): 43–58.

Pratt, Jane. "The Anne Frank We Remember," In *McCall's* (January 1986): 72.

Pommer, Henry F. "The Legend and Art of Anne Frank," In *Judaism* 9 (1960): 36–46.

Schnabel, Ernst. *Anne Frank: A Portrait in Courage*. New York: Harcourt Brace, 1958.

Small, Michael. "Miep Gies, Who Hid Anne Frank, Adds a Coda to the Famous Diary," *People Weekly* 29:15 (April 18, 1988): 123.

Steenmeiher, Anna G., ed., with Otto Frank and Henri van Praag. *A Tribute to Anne Frank*. Garden City, NY: Doubleday, 1971.

van der Rol, Ruud, and Rian Verhoeven. *Anne Frank: Beyond the Diary: A Photographic Remembrance*. New York: Puffin Books, 1993.

van Galen Last, Dick. *Anne Frank and After*. Amsterdam: Amsterdam University Press, 1996.

Van Maarsen, Jackqueline. *My Friend Anne Frank*. New York: Vantage Press, 1996.

Western, Richard D. "The Case for Anne Frank: The Diary of a Young Girl," In *Celebrating Censored Books*. Nicholas J. Karolides and Lee Burress, ed. ERIC, 1985. 12–14.

Wiebe, Philip. "Anne Frank," *Welt der Arbeit* (World of Work) (April 29, 1955): 3.

Wiesenthal, Simon. "Epilogue to Anne Frank's Diary," In *The Murderers Among Us: The Simon Wiesenthal Memoirs*. Joseph Wechsberg, ed. New York: McGraw-Hill, 1967. 171–83.

Wilson, Matthew. "The Ghost Writer: Kafka, Het Achterhuis, and History," In *Studies in American Jewish Literature* 10:1 (Spring 1991): 44–53.

Other Media:

Anne Frank Remembered (Videocassette). Sony Pictures Classics, 1995.

The Attic: The Hiding of Anne Frank (Videocassette). Great Britain: Yorkshire Television Enterprises, 1988.

Avenue of the Just (Videocassette). New York: Anti-Defamation League.

The Man Who Hid Anne Frank (Videocassette). Canadian Broadcasting System, 1980.

The World of Anne Frank (Videocassette). Teaneck, NJ: Ergo Media, Inc., 1987.

Acknowledgments

"The Ignored Lesson of Anne Frank" by Bruno Bettelheim from *Harper's* (November 1960): 45–50, reprinted in *Surviving and Other Essays* by Bruno Bettelheim. Copyright © 1979 by Bruno Bettelheim and Trude Bettelheim as Trustees.

"The Americanization of the Holocaust on Stage and Screen" by Lawrence L. Langer from *From Hester Street to Hollywood: The Jewish-American Stage and Screen*, Sarah Blacher Cohen, ed. Copyright © 1983 by Indiana University Press.

"Growing Up Banished: A Reading of Anne Frank and Etty Hillesum" by Yasmine Ergas from *Behind the Lines: Gender and the Two World Wars*, Margaret Randolph Higonnet, Jane Jenson, Sonya Michel, and Margaret Collins Weitz, eds. Copyright © 1987 by Yale University Press.

"The Dead Child Speaks: Reading *The Diary of Anne Frank*" by Sander L. Gilman from *Studies in American Jewish Literature* 7:1 (Spring 1988). Copyright ©1988 by The Kent State University Press.

"Anne Frank's Reading" by Sylvia Patterson Iskander from *Children's Literature Association Quarterly* 13:3 (Fall 1988): 137–41. Copyright © 1988 by Southwest Texas State University.

"Anne Frank's Autobiographical Style" by Sylvia Patterson Iskander from *Children's Literature Association Quarterly* 16:2 (Summer 1991): 78–81. Copyright © 1991 by Southwest Texas State University.

Index